Bláthanna

Irish Spaces in Flower

First published in 2019 by

Carrowmore

6-9 Trinity Street

Dublin 2

Ireland

www.carrowmore.ie

© Ruth Monahan, Ultan Devaney, Kasia Skopińska, 2019

www.appassionata.ie

9781999323400

British Library Cataloguing in Publication Data

An entry can be found on request

Library of Congress Cataloging in Publication Data

An entry can be found on request

Design by WorkGroup

Typeset in Freight

1

Bláthanna

Irish Spaces in Flower

Ruth Monahan, Kasia Skopińska, Ultan Devaney

Contents

Ruth Monahan

Hailing from Sligo, Ruth graduated from Dublin City University with a thesis on *The Simpsons* and a first-class degree before she went on to achieve a Masters in Multimedia from Trinity College Dublin. She worked for over ten years in television production before joining McQueen's London to study and work in floral design. In 2004 she co-founded Appassionata Flowers with her then partner and now husband, Ultan.

Ruth is the face, drive and energy behind our company, Appassionata Flowers. She loves raspberries and marmalade, the colour orange, and does cry during films. Her love of flowers and gardening comes from her Granny Monahan, her love of fashion from her Nana Doyle. She is Mum to Maya and Roman, two special florists in waiting – even though they don't know it yet.

Kasia Skopińska

Kasia's early family life saw her immersed in nature from a very young age, having grown up on a flower farm in Poland. Lucky to be part of a third generation flower growing legacy, the nascent seeds (pun intentional) had been firmly planted.

Kasia has a M.Sc. in Horticulture, Plant Protection and Dendrology. Her studies built upon the depth of knowledge garnered from early exposure to all things flora, that would carry her all the way from Poland to Ireland and into the Appassionata family. Kasia is the Creative Director at Appassionata and has been living her best flower life for twelve years and counting!

Kasia can be found most weekends at the allotment or swimming in the Irish Sea. She loves dancing, hates onions, and often loses her wallet.

Ultan Devaney

Ultan Devaney is Sligo born and bred. He studied Media Studies at the University of Ulster, was a Students' Union Site President and holds an MBA from the Smurfit School of Business in Dublin. Ultan worked in television in camera and sound production in Ireland and worldwide before co-founding Appassionata Flowers fifteen years ago. As chief financial officer, he also shoulders responsibility for HR and all things technical within the company. A triathlete, and a lover of music with a fondness for his own homemade granola, he is also an eager mixologist. He is a father to Maya and Roman, whom he loves to hang out with, but he is beginning to cramp their style.

Sean Breithaupt and Yvette Monahan

Sean Breithaupt and Yvette Monahan are two photographers who came together to collaborate on this beautiful book. They are also married to each other.

Sean works predominantly in the design, advertising and editorial realm, providing a visual narrative for a variety of clients and features.

Yvette is a photographic artist; her practice looks to create images that reflect the inner world and outer spaces. She has exhibited and published her images widely.

We were prompted to make a book about the flower world we weave after an impromptu phone call on a winter's day from Maeve and Stephanie, both of whom work in publishing, who thought we might be interested in capturing our floral work in a book. Kasia and I (Ruth) have worked together for over thirteen years now, and have often mused on the idea of making pieces that we loved, taking them as far as our sense of play would allow. Ultan, the practical member of our flower business, gradually joined our thinking about this book journey, too.

Bláthanna means 'flowers' in the Irish language. We wanted to curate a series of floral short stories in Irish spaces. This anthology is a selection box that exhibits our playful work with flowers. We chose spaces, some well known, some we just loved, some we found along the way – but all of which inspired us as we started to piece together which flowers would work in each space. Each chapter showcases our flower stylings and delves into the histories, mythologies, legends, and flower meanings that led us to create in each location.

We have drawn from Irish countryside textures, native gardens, and flowers from here in Ireland and around the globe, allowing them to shape our responses to each special surrounding. Each chapter marks the end of a journey where we often had a finished result that differed from what we had planned on sketched paper. But that is the joy of working with flowers. It is a part of the process when working with such wonderful ingredients that we are often led to produce unintentional work that, nevertheless, is meant to be.

Our work brings us into the bowels of many buildings; we get to create floral artistry and dress lots of places that most eyes never get to see. And so we thought that we should make use of this privilege and have some floral adventures, drawing up a wish list of wonderful spots we wanted to make flower displays in for you all to experience. We never expected to have such a soul-searching journey in our flower work, nor did we think that we would meet so many interesting people, who belong to, and mind, these Irish spaces. We also experienced every form of Irish weather, relearning how to just go with a spontaneous, perfectly poised cloud formation, and how to appreciate the sheer effort of holding a structure on a sand dune for an hour in sporadic, sunny gusts. Much of this book was almost a reignition of appreciation for this island we live on and the personality to be found in locations all over the country.

It was such a feeling of indulgence to be able to choose whichever flowers we wanted and to have the time to play around with various ideas. What was so interesting for us was that, no matter where we went, our flowers had such an impact on everyone who, by virtue of being there, was able to preview our productions.

We are always conscious of how flowers affect the person who receives them; our work means that we celebrate all of life's cyclical wonders in the rollercoaster that is our time spent on Earth. However, it is all too easy to become complacent about flowers, their colours and forms, their seasons and origins, in the everyday floristry that is a part of the work we do. This book has brought light and delight back into our work with blooms, and has reinforced the privileged and lucky position we have in being able to work with such beauty each day. A florist is someone who is addicted to flowers – to all the nature that they bring and the inspiration that they give us. All we need to do now is mind this precious world that they grow in so that we can keep binding, weaving, building, making, and loving what we do in Irish spaces.

It is not often that you get to work with two of your favourite friends in the world. One of them being Kasia Skopińska, originally from Poland, who has made our island her fond home and has worked alongside me for over thirteen years. Our symbiotic relationship is such that we came up with the same ideas for each spot, and were able to laugh each time something went wrong. It was so special to honour Kasia's native Kupala tradition in this book, and to have her background as a flower grower inform so many of the stories we made. And then Ultan, my husband in life and in flowers, whose practical head and physical strength meant that we could create the ideas myself and Kasia drew up on a page. Whether it was holding a currach for five hours in Glendalough or suspending Tetris flowers on the surface of the RHA, each shoot was a cross-training workshop for him.

And as for me, Ruth, this book marks a new stage in our flower-making life. I originally began life as a florist over fifteen years ago, starting Appassionata Flowers in a small cottage kitchen. Never did I imagine then that we would get the chance to create the flower ideas that follow in these pages, allowing us to show them off to you, the reader. I think being a florist is a vocation: the flowers pull you in. I am so lucky to walk into our studio, our shops, and to be accosted by colour, scent, and seasons, and work with flowers every day. This book has definitely made me appreciate the wonderful world we weave, and the fact that, no matter what else might be going on, a deep nosedive into a scented wrap of blooms will make all the worries go away.

And then we had the joy of working alongside Yvette, my sister, and her husband Sean, whose craft as photographers, already so strongly recognised, made this book what it is. Yes, we brought the flowers, the ideas, and we organised for them to come to every location we had in mind. But it is their vision, their skill behind the lens, and their advice that has brought all of our ideas into the beautiful life and reality of the images found in this book. Their patience with us was unfounded, their enthusiasm for what we were trying to do, amazing. They are superstars.

We couldn't have created this book without the backup and the blessing of our incredible Appassionata team. This sixteen-month adventure in blooms could not have been made a reality without every single one of you – you helped in so many ways. Nothing was a problem, whether it was driving back and forth many times to where we were trying to be or if we needed some help with the making on a mad busy day in the studio. And a big thank you to Lynn, who held the fort while while Kasia, Ultan and I were consumed with photographing flowers. Can we just say a million thanks to you all, because you are all so brilliant and we love you loads.

We are hugely grateful for all of the wonderful spaces and places we were given the opportunity to work in, and we particularly appreciate the people who mind them for letting us play flowers there for hours. It has been so wonderful to meet you all, and we hope that you love the flowers we arranged in the places that you so care for. A special mention to Brian Matthews, who, through his gardening world and love of unusual locations, brought us to visit the most magical spots, and his suggestions and help throughout this book were invaluable.

And last but not least, myself and Ultan's children, Maya and Roman. Your patience with your parents as they were 'doing a flower book' was remarkable, and we promise you that next year we won't be bringing you to random spots in Ireland to hang out whilst we stand, stop, stare, and start again on each installation we make. You are both amazing and we love you so much.

A note from Ultan

Over the past sixteen months, friends and family have asked two questions: What's your book about? Why are you compiling a book? I hope what you now hold in your hands explains what we were doing in a way that I never could.

Nevertheless, the question of 'why' was always a little harder to answer. Even given the most optimistic of predictions, it was not for any potential financial reward. Neither was it to fill idle hands.

When running your own business, rewards are complicated. Winning a new contract, nailing a pitch, completing a client's requirements, your team's smiles of relief once a difficult job has been perfectly executed – it all keeps you going. But nothing touches working for yourselves. Truly working for ourselves and each other. Challenging your own ability and ideas; giving it a go and putting it out there so there's nowhere to hide. Why? I don't really have a good answer to that, but this has been one of the most rewarding adventures yet.

A note from Kasia

I have been told many times before not to complain about the Irish weather since choosing to live here. Therefore, not only will I not complain, I will admit that those dark, moody skies, perfect cloud formations, the sideways rain and forever green fields made me (and many others) feel at home.

To be invited to join Ruth and Ultan on this project was mind-blowing. Thinking outside of the box, and realising there was no box, was a joy. No place was too far, no idea was too strange.

Within the constant conversation, some questions stood out: Can we do it? How will we do it? If we could, where would we do it?

Our journey began as we set sail in September of 2018. Suddenly we had a currach filled with flowers out on the mysterious, dark waters of Glendalough. We made a wish and let the water kindly carry our boat of blooms. What the currach became was more than we could have imagined, both in terms of the work put into making it (standing in a freezing cold lake does make a person question their sanity), and in terms of how many accidental but wonderful surprises we discovered along the way.

The currach scene beautifully prefigures our journey through Irish spaces. Excitement and a spirited anxiety were constant companions that we learned to embrace during the making of this book. It was a humbling experience to weave flowers into already beautiful landscapes, homes, and buildings in the hope of achieving something harmonious.

Bláthanna: Irish Spaces in Flower

The Fumbally

Happenings in green

Fumbally Lane, Dublin 8

'This is the place of creative incubation. At first, you may find nothing happens there. But, if you have a sacred place and use it, take advantage of it, something will happen.'

Joseph Campbell
Extract from *The Power of Myth*

One day we went to play flowers in the Fumbally Stables in the Liberties, Co. Dublin. What we wanted was an empty, interesting room in which to toy with textures, stems, and ingredients that sometimes get hidden as accessory elements or minor touches. Every florist loves to forage, especially in autumn, but every florist also loves to work with green, be it leaf, plant, or stem. The stables gave us the stage with which to express our love of simplicity.

This space, a sister to the Fumbally café, was created by Luca D'Alfonso and Aisling Rogerson, who bared the partition walls, suspended ceilings, and brick arches, preserving as many original features as possible so that the stables allowed for people to create their own space. This building was constructed some time around 1750, and was originally a stable for the nearby breweries and distilleries in Blackpitts. It has evolved over the years: at various times a meat factory, a bakery, a photography studio, and now simply a space to breathe.

And so on a warm August day we brought along ferns to act as flowers, passion flower that refused to flower, aquatic plants that were all dried out, and food in the shape of flowers. With this, we began.

A little vanity project, but we could not make a book without mentioning the flower 'flora appassionata', which started our journey in the world of blooms. The language of flowers describes this long climber garland of green, which only popped one bloom on this particular day, as 'Fervent Devotion'. This astonishing flower is a festival unto itself. A crucifix-shaped, yellow stamen surrounded by filaments and petals in pinks, whites, purple, and red, with long, slender, curling leaves and slinky spring tendrils, puts this bloom at a great remove from the ordinary. It is considered a miraculous flower, which, in warmer European climes, carries fleshy fruit for the whole summer. The flora appassionata not only inspired our name, but perfectly describes the devotion we bring to our work in the world of flowers.

We simply created a curtain with a meandering but definite drop, falling in curls to the concrete floor. Sunlight shone, distilling an effervescence in the passion flower which might be missed if it was simply used as a garland accessory in summer. The delicacy of hanging each lengthy strand so that the drape allowed a see-through effect resulted in a waterfall of wonder – even when we couldn't find that single flowering bloom in the end!

An ode to asparagus fern

If green was the new black, a mix-up of asparagus ferns would star in every show. Despite not being a fern or a vegetable, this climber is not only celebrating a seventies comeback, dressing the homes of everyone we know, it also has powers to clear the air around us. This 'fern' is so named as its fronds look like the top of an asparagus stalk, yet it is actually related to the lily family and spreads by seed rather than spore. These plants are rife with sentimentality for Kasia, as her family used to grow them commercially during her Polish childhood, before they became part of the current greening-up-your-home oeuvre.

Whether it's the lacy frothiness, the glossiness, the jade fuzziness of the various varieties, or just the idea that these plants will last for years, this plant is full of contradictions. Considered a thing of beauty in Europe, natives to New Zealand and Hawaii call it an invasive weed. However, we are fans of its earthiness, the textures, and the way these plants can make an installation sing.

Sheaves of various types of ferns were loaded on to the antique trolley before they were bound into a hanging celebration of themselves. The rustic, wheeled cart waited patiently for us to finish procrastinating with our passion flower but, while resting, created a pretty picture where each frond detail could be admired. Shades of green pulsated in the light, making shadows as the different stem details collectively created the drama of an explosion. As often happens in our work, sometimes we just sit things down before the creativity begins and find something has already been answered; the piled stems sat perfectly in this instance, looking like they were meant to be there all along.

The tall, irregular Long Room wall textures drew light from facing windows. We stood on stepladders, filling up the empty chicken wire wound around a birch trunk. Bunches and clutches of ferns were placed in layers to create a luxurious look, a play of dark and deep, a mix of leaf styles coming together as one.

We placed two square stools in front of the 'ode to fern' piece and created a staged moment for a couple's celebration of all cultures, cementing a simple green ceremony in time. There was a simple stillness about it all as the sunlight bounced, moved, delighted, and changed the shades of green in the fern garland hanging so peacefully.

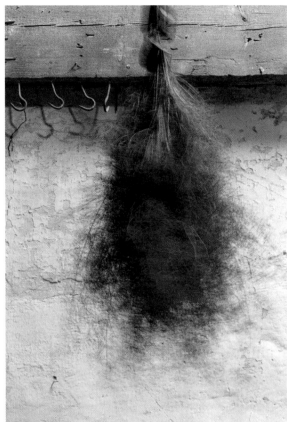

A historical hook

Perhaps the hook that hung in the space was from its time as a bakery or distillery, but hanging dried water plantain from it was too tempting to miss. The water plantain used is an Irish wildflower that is typically found growing on the sides of canals, so it was apt to have it bring its dried beauty along to a building near the Grand Canal. The starkness of the plantain's dried form matched the patched, elderly wall; the brutality of the curved hook, probably meant for metal buckets to bring to the wooden door above, held this foraged foliage for a photo that stole our hearts.

Some flower food

The Fumbally Stables is also home to a special kitchen where the café team educate, ferment, distil, and create new ways to work with food, for themselves and for their customers and community. We thought that this space's essence would lend itself to an exhibition of how flowers have been used over the centuries, both in landscaping and as a food source, especially given the current resurgence in Irish food culture. We created a set of minimal, single-flower vase displays, each with beautiful stems that can actually be considered as food in its first form, as found in a growing field.

These architectural, minimal displays were each bound and manipulated into a clean stem spiral, the basis of all floristry technique – a mono-flower, single-stem display requires perfection, or the impact can be lost. Placed side by side, the flowers can lose context and simply seem a truncated grouping, but once we look at each vase's individual contents, the idea of flowers becoming the food of life becomes clear.

Flowers

Water plantain – *Alisma plantago-aquatica* (Irish: corrchopóg)

Water plantain is native to Ireland and can be found growing on the margins of canals. This wildflower can grow to one metre in height and produces pale-lilac, three-petalled, rounded flowers. It is also said to have curative properties.

Artichoke – *Cynara scolymus* (Irish: bliosán gréine cruinne)

The globe artichoke and its punky, psychedelic-purple, spiky fronds is not only an heirloom vegetable, grown so that the tender flower buds can be dipped into hollandaise sauce – its very appearance, so architectural in shape, lends itself to a very contemporary-looking garden patch. It is a close relative of the thistle.

Quinoa – *Chenopodium quinoa* (Irish: cuineo)

This protein-packed seed, the main crop of the Andes, was initially cultivated by the Incas, going back to 3000 BC. Now a superfood, this delicate-scented, herbaceous annual plant grows up to two metres in height, and can be harvested each autumn for a wonderful quinoa stew, muesli, or salad. The good news is that this crop can grow easily in the Irish climate – here's to seeing it coming closer to home.

**Korean angelica – *Angelica gigas*
(Irish: allfheabhrán)**

An umbellifer, this very medicinal, herbaceous
plant is full of attitude and personality. This purple
version originated in Korea and is grown there as
an aphrodisiac, but here the stems and roots can
be used in all sorts of cooking due to its parsnip-
like taste and texture. Traditionally in Ireland, the
cow's parsley-like angelica grows on roadsides,
and would have been considered an antidote
to poisons and a protection against witches.

**Salad burnet – *Sanguisorba
minor* (Irish: lus an uille)**

This flower brings great joy with its tight,
pink, fluffy puff bloom. In a garden, it wafts
through the wind in a lovely way, like a gauze.
All insects and bees love it. The flowers taste
delicious in a salad, and they have a hint of
cucumber if placed in a summer drink. We are
planning to dry loads of them for home, too.

Flowers used in Fumbally Stables

- Artichoke – *Cynara scolymus*
  (Irish: bliosán gréine cruinne)
- Asparagus fern – *Asparagus aethiopicus*
  (Irish: fearn/raithneach mhór)
- Emerald fern – *Asparagus sprengeri*
  (Irish: raithneach iathghlas)
- Forest asparagus – *Asparagus
  falcatus* (Irish: raithneach chrua)
- Foxtail fern – *Asparagus densiflorus*
  (Irish: fearn/raithneach sionnaigh)

- Korean angelica – *Angelica
  gigas* (Irish: allfheabhrán)
- Passion flower – *Passiflora
  caerulea* (Irish: bláth paisean)
- Quinoa – *Chenopodium
  quinoa* (Irish: cuineo)
- Salad burnet – *Sanguisorba
  minor* (Irish: lus an uille)
- Umbrella Fern – *Asparagus umbellatus*
- Water plantain– *Alisma plantago-
  aquatica* (Irish: corrchopóg)

Mullaghmore

A Mullaghmore light melody

County Sligo

'And the season is at its cusp. The moment will soon drop its weight to summer.'

Kevin Barry

Extract from *Beatlebone*

We made a table of spring transitioning to summer in Mullaghmore, Co. Sligo. Our intention was to make you feel that you were lying in sunlight, in all its varying movements, along the Dartry Mountains from dawn until dusk. A colourful range of pharmacy bottles filled with a meadow of bold brightness disrupted the long winter and grey-spring feeling on that particular shoot day.

Mullaghmore in north Sligo is a fishing village nestled on a dramatic peninsula, pinched by the almost Disney-like Classiebawn Castle. 'Mullagh', as we call it, or '*An Mhullach Mór*' in Irish, has a big hill up to the fishermen's houses, built in the eighteenth century; as a child, you knew you were getting fit when you could run up that hill at the end of August in fully soaked clothing, a result of lifesaving classes that took place during Irish Water Safety week.

It's a place where the headland is walked daily and fans of flora search for bright-pink sea thrift, irises, and famous orchids hiding behind hills. There's a rocky inlet called Bishop's Pool where a bishop used to bathe amidst the kelp and sea spaghetti. Years before, fields stood full of drying stacks of seaweed, and children jumped off of round haystacks with glee before they were spotted and had to scramble over lichen-heavy stone walls to get home. At the time, peat and smoke filled the air, and whitewashed cottages, with families that went back generations, had their yellow half-doors left ajar. Shrimp were caught as tides turned by standing with a large net at the harbour mouth. On nights of spring tide, children would dare each other to climb the stone harbour steps and jump into the sea for a thrill. This village makes rose-tinted summer holidays a reality. Families from Sligo and the North have gone on holiday here for generations, and still do.

The summer home we're in is on top of a hill overlooking a long, sandy beach ending at Mermaid's Cove. From here we have views of the Atlantic, the heights of Slieve League, Donegal town and, in our own back garden, Kings Mountain. As the sun roams across cloud formations in the sky's open vista, the sea can change from glistening blue, as if mermaids are twinkling below, to monochrome greys and whites within a moment. Gusts and rainfall can be spotted from miles out, which helps in planning ahead for any wonderful walks. Kings Mountain's personality morphs from solid limestone to a creviced-green starkness, sometimes disappearing completely when cloud cover comes down to play.

This summer home of wetsuits, walking, fishing, and family plays host to many a meal at the dining table in the kitchen. Guests gather and look at the view, dinners run on for hours, and everyone tries to take photos of the moon and stars, because the house is far beyond city lights; the twinkling sky is all we can see at night.

A view of the Atlantic, Sligo, Donegal Bay, and a meadow – seemingly ordinary, but at the same time extraordinary, because we crave it during our stays at the seaside. We decided to create a contemporary, low meadow lane on our dining table, one like the lane behind the house that leads on to the cliff walk and the vast ocean. The display had to sit below the eyeline so that the flowers and panorama could coexist. The dining table became a metaphor for the play of light during the day.

Bláthanna: Irish Spaces in Flower

Taking still photos over the course of a day allows us see how the flowers' personalities blossom. The poppies definitely provided the most thrills; their papery textured petals and fragrant centres unfurled, moved, opened, and altered as light and temperature oscillated from morning to night.

This was the weekend of bluebells; we found carpets of them wherever we walked. Despite this, bluebells arrived with us from Poland, so we didn't have to disturb the magic carpets of woodland blue that surrounded. Poppies were literally popping out of every roadside, and sea thrift hadn't arrived so we used scabiosa. Peonies resembled the colour of sea urchins collected during sea dives around Thumb Rock in the seventies; protea added that coral-like feel of all that lies beneath the Classiebawn cliffs; anemones and sweet pea gave that height-of-summer brightness, even though it was still April. As we styled each of the pharmacy bottles, making a kaleidoscope in bloom, we smelled the strong scent of each stem.

Taking still photos over the course of a day allows us see how the flowers' personalities blossom. The poppies definitely provided the most thrills; their papery textured petals and fragrant centres unfurled, moved, opened, and altered as light and temperature oscillated from morning to night. You could almost imagine everyone standing around the table while eating so as not to destroy the scene – but sooner or later we might have needed some space to place a glass after some summer wine.

Flowers

Bluebell - *Hyacinthoides non-scripta* (Irish: coinnle corra)

The bluebell is an iconic image of the Irish countryside, with its delicate, deep-blue flowers carpeting our wild woods in late spring and early summer. It is always wonderful to walk through this carpet in hues of blue as sunlight sparkles in woodlands around us. It is a member of the lily family and it is a symbol of beauty in Irish myth. One myth states that Fionn and his men were put to sleep with bluebell mixture to allow Gráinne to elope with Diarmuid. The sap has been used to glue books, set tail feathers on arrows, and cure throat ailments.

Poppy - *Papaver* (Irish: cailleach)

The Irish for the bud of the poppy is *cocán*. *'Mar chocán ar chnocán lá gréine'*, translates to 'as a poppy on a height on a summer's day', meaning something beautiful. Wild poppies have been used in folk medicine as painkillers for toothache, earache and to cure coughs.

Anemone - *Anemone nemorosa* (Irish: lus na gaoithe)

These flowers add a playful touch to any floral piece, with their inset eyes amidst large petals of block colours, usually in purple, reds, punky pinks, and whites. They come from the buttercup family, like delphinium and ranunculus, and they are named after the Greek for 'God of the Wind'. Their leaves are said to alleviate headaches when boiled in water.

Flowers used on dining table

- Anemone 'Pink Hanoi Mistral' – *Anemone nemorosa* (Irish: lus na gaoithe)
- Bluebell - *Hyacinthoides non-scripta* (Irish: coinnle corra)
- Clematis – *Clematis* (Irish: cleimeatas)
- Fringed Tulip – *Tulipa*
- Peony 'Red Charm' – *Paeonia* (Irish: piaine)
- Poppy – *Papaver rhoeas* (Irish: ailleach dhearg)
- Protea Waratah – *Telopea speciosissima* (Irish: unknown, trópaiceach)
- Scabiosa columbaria 'Butterfly Blue' – *Scabiosa columbaria* (Irish: cab an ghasáin)
- Sweet pea 'Misty Apricot' (Irish: peasairin)
- Sweet pea 'Misty Pinkwave'
- Sweet pea 'Winter Sunshine White'
- Sweet pea 'Misty Rosy Red'
- Sweet pea 'Candy Scoop'
- Sweet pea 'Marshmallow Scoop'
- Sweet pea 'At Revel Scoop'
- Rose 'David Austin Amazing London' – *Rosa* (Irish: rós)
- Rose 'David Austin Beatrice'

King's Inns

A stairwell of smoke bush

Henrietta Place, Dublin 1

The summer of the smoke bush

We called it the summer of the smoke bush: 2018 was the year of the hottest summer on record in Ireland. One advantage of the temperature rise was that it made the cotinus so sumptuous and overscale. It is usually only available in southern Europe and Australia (we are always envious of the Australian florists' smoke bush hauls) so you can imagine our florista excitement when this woolly, frothy shrub was easily within reach.

Smoke bush gets its common name from its large flower plumes, which look like a puff of brown or pinkish smoke over their foliage in late summer and early autumn. Some bushes have so many flower heads that the whole bush looks like a cloud of smoke, yet others do not smoke much – or at all – and are grown for their beautiful foliage. Either way, it is a truly wonderful thing.

A staircase seed is planted

For years, we have had the pleasure of dressing King's Inns each week and filling it with flowers that reflect our respect for its various spaces. Over the years working here, we started to notice the moodiness of the interior, the play of shadows through small windows, the secret stairways to hidden rooms. We wanted to make a story that matched the building's grandeur and ghostliness with an ethereal flower piece.

We started with the entrance urns, thinking that 1,500 stems of that summer's cotinus clouds – enormous domes – would match the copper details, but might overwhelm the grandeur of the situation. Though we arranged the smoke bush in abundant structures that were huge in dimension, the stature of the building's stone columns reduced them considerably. We enjoyed the creative licence of using just one texture to create an impact, even if we were the only souls there that day to witness it.

From there, the stairwell took shape. We wove the cotinus as if it was a lava cloud, spilling and expanding like dripping oil as it descended the steps from the Bench Room upstairs. Thousands of stems stood, bent, bounded, and bounced, and made long meringue-shaped clouds. The ethereal hues of copper and blush suggested a beauty and lightness that perfectly juxtaposed the minimal interior lighting and the stairs' bare stone steps, which so many judges and lawmakers have climbed.

Smoke bush gets its common name from its large flower plumes, which look like a puff of brown or pinkish smoke over their foliage in late summer and early autumn. Some bushes have so many flower heads that the whole bush looks like a cloud of smoke, yet others do not smoke much – or at all – and are grown for their beautiful foliage. Either way, it is a truly wonderful thing.

All about why we love King's Inns

The Honorable Society of King's Inns is the oldest institution of legal education in Ireland, and plays an important part in the making of Appassionata's flower life. Firstly, it is James Gandon's final building, located in the centre of Dublin, and designed in the early 1800s. When you approach the front entrance, you are met with a grand vista. There is the elegant centre with two wings, the central cupola, which forms a gorgeous arched gateway, and the beautiful copper-domed roof detail. The principal front faces on to Constitution Hill, but we always enter from the remarkable Henrietta Street, through the large gateway. We can sense the movement of history each time we pass through that street; as far as Irish streets are concerned, it is the single most intact and important architectural collection of houses from early eighteenth-century Georgian times. This street began as the primary residence of those in power in the worlds of religion, law, and banking; it then transformed from townhouses into tenement buildings, and is now considered a cultural phenomenon, reborn as a memento to our social and architectural history.

As we enter through the large, heavy doors of the front entrance, carrying crates of flowers, we are met by the grand staircase, flanked by pillars and urns, and witness Edward Smyth's caryatides – supporting columns sculpted in the form of draped female figures – which support the cornices, carved to represent the theme of wine and plenty. They mark the doorway to the historic Dining Hall, where many men and women have dined, wed, partied, and sung under the gaze of those men sitting and staring from the gilded frames of their portraits. We were so inspired to finally create a cotinus cascade on the steps we had climbed so many times, and wished that everyone could see this architectural gem, a hidden bastion of the world of law.

Flowers

Smoke bush – *Cotinus coggygria* (Irish: tor atá faoi bhláth/tor bláthanna)

This unusual shrub gets its name from the billowy hairs attached to the elongated stalks on the spent flower clusters. In summer, these hairs alter in graduated shades of smoky to purplish pink, and this creates a tree covering of fluffy, hazy, smoke-like, puffy clouds. It is native to a large part of the globe, from southern Europe, east across central Asia and the Himalayas, to northern China. We usually only get to use smoke bush for a month a year, maximum, so this shoot in King's Inns was so special for us that day.

Carrowmore

A flower gate of folklore where the land meets the sky

Cúil Irra Peninsula, County Sligo

'The wind has bundled up the clouds high over Knocknarea,
And thrown the thunder on the stones for all that Maeve can say.
Angers that are like noisy clouds have set our hearts abeat;
But we have all bent low and low and kissed the quiet feet
Of Cathleen, the daughter of Houlihan.'

W.B. Yeats

Extract from 'Red Hanrahan's Song About Ireland'

Building a hedgerow-style gate where the land meets the sea brings on a togetherness for our flower frolics in Sligo. Hawthorn, or whitethorn, was exploding around us that weekend, its white blossom bursting to tell everyone that spring had finally sprung. Native to Ireland, this bushy tree marks field boundaries and loves to hang around an archaeological site. Farmers leave it alone, as it is known as 'fairy thorn'; it is considered bad luck from the fairies if cut down, and has the magical power to last four hundred years. Don't worry, we minded this superstition, but we did order spirea to masquerade as hawthorn in order to create an ode to a stunning stone circle.

And of course serendipity would have it that we found a wonderful hedgerow beside the most perfect passage tomb in Carrowmore, which looks directly on Queen Maeve, herself buried in an unexcavated cairn on top of Knocknarea, and is frowned upon by Benbulben across the bay. 'Carrowmore 7', as it is known, is a perfect dolmen surrounded by a full circle of stones; it is a favourite in this great megalithic complex of ancient Ireland. The view was made especially exceptional as no sign of modern living – electricity wires, poles, or indeed houses – is visible as you look through this stone-framed space.

Feeling the forces of nature, mythology, and legend as a gale blew around us, we ended up making two horizontal gates with a spring countryside feeling to channel the *Fir Bolg*, warriors who were buried here after their battle in Moytura. We wanted to invite those legendary folk in. We also wanted to honour Queen Maeve, who still stands fully armoured, facing Ulster, under 40,000 stones. We left a bunch of Irish lily of the valley at Carrowmore 7 to say thank you to the little folk for letting us play flowers in their field.

The magnitude of the moving air and the wobbliness of the Neolithic field surface made us work at a pace, firstly by creating a foliaged structure with winter skimmia (to say goodbye to that season) and Irish eucalyptus (for a fragrant frolic). Bunches and buckets were brought down a field lane, carried over barbed wire fences, and chased after, as the wind stole stems constantly and blew them down the field.

Each side of the gate had to match perfectly to mirror the tomb's symmetry, so masterfully made in Neolithic times. Spirea and Queen Anne's lace piled in, frothing in the waves of wind. Then we added in fiery crocosmia, asclepias, and deep, furied red astilbe in a nod to the strength and prowess of Queen Maeve, standing tall and proud on her mountain above us. The delicate but silently strong blue delphinium and nigella were added in to illustrate our awe of the local sky and sea.

We had to catch our breath after laughing so much at the madness of our flower-making situation, but we also marvelled at the ancient, magical landscape our gate opened on to, marking an end to our north-western adventure in blooms.

Carrowmore

Knocknarea and Queen Maeve

Here lies one of the greatest megalithic complexes of ancient Ireland, *An Cheathrú Mhór*, or Carrowmore as we call it today: the Irish name means 'The Great Quarter'. Spread over a plateau of some one hundred and fifty acres and centred on the high point of Listoghil, there are thirty recognisable tomb sites but it is suggested that there were once at least a hundred monuments here. New information from DNA suggests that the monuments were built and used by people who came by sea from France around six thousand years ago. It is said that they brought the first cattle to Ireland, and that they also reintroduced native red deer here after their post-Ice Age Irish extinction.

Legend has it that the *Fir Bolg* – considered one of the greatest Celtic tribes; rulers of Ireland before the *Tuatha Dé Danann* arrived – are buried here. Their name translating to 'belly men', the interior of the megalithic passage tombs was designed to resemble a womb or belly – the shaft of light from the outside sky touched the cremated bones of ancestors to continue the cycle of life.

This large hill, known as 'Hill of the Kings', is carpeted in heather; at the summit lies a chambered cairn. It stands proudly, in Yeats's words, as the symbol of 'The Land of Heart's Desire', and is located some four kilometres west of Carrowmore, between the bays of Sligo and Ballisodare, on the Cúil Irra peninsula. Made of limestone, this hill, 327 metres in elevation, is visually striking as a mound-shaped monolith, and was a major place of ritual and meeting in the Neolithic era.

Journalist William Bulfin, one of Ireland's first bicycle tourists, was also enchanted by Knocknarea, writing in his book *Rambles in Éirinn* (1907):

The mountain has no partner in its glory ... And about Knocknarea itself lies an epic suggestiveness which you cannot miss if you climb the mountain. You cannot keep your hold on the present while you are up there.

The impressive chambered cairn is 200 feet in length, 40 feet in height. It is said to hold Queen Maeve – an unexcavated passage tomb, but filled with feminist power. Maeve was the Queen of Connacht and her legendary life fuelled many a fairy tale, myth, and story. Even Shakespeare was inspired by her for *Romeo and Juliet* when Mercutio says, 'O, then I see Queen Mab hath been with you. She is the fairies' midwife.' The tomb is believed to date to around 3000 BCE.

Flowers

**Hawthorn – *Crataegus monogyna*
(Irish: sceach gheal)**

From mid-May, our Irish fields and hedgerows
burst alive with clusters of tiny, white,
beautiful flowers, which happily mark the end
of a dark winter for us all. This is hawthorn.
As a spiny-branched, small tree, each of its
tiny, twelve-millimetre blooms combines to
create a sense of dancing white delicacy all
around our countryside. The direct translation
from Irish means 'bright' or 'radiant'. Most
importantly for any foragers out there, it is
considered such bad luck to cut it down.

**Lily of the valley – *Convallaria
majalis* (Irish: lily an ghleann)**

A delicate, dainty woodland flower with a scent
that exceeds its size. Irish lore has it that they
formed ladders for fairies so that they could reach
reeds with which to plait their cradles; as such,
we felt they were more than fitting to leave as a
token of our thanks that day in the fairy field.

Astilbe – *Astilbe arendsii*

The astilbe flower is also known as false spirea,
false goat's beard, and feather flower. It is
said to carry the meaning 'I will be waiting
for you' or 'I'll still be waiting', symbolising
patience and dedication to a loved one.

Nigella – *Nigella damascena* (Irish: nigéal)

Also known as love-in-a-mist, it is a member of
the buttercup/ranunculus family. This flower is so
much hardier than it looks, and was appropriate to
wave at the Queen herself. Nigella was traditionally
planted to attract love and to represent the
strong feminine power of an alluring woman.

**Queen Anne's lace – *Ammi
majus* (Irish: umbalaigh)**

A member of the wild carrot family, Queen Anne's
lace is a well-known sight along our country
roads in early summer. Sometimes it is called
cow parsley and it was traditionally placed
on May altars to honour the Virgin Mary.

Milkweed – *Asclepias* (Irish: buinneachan)

A perfect food for butterflies. With its
pretty, orange mini-flowers, milkweed was
known as sun spurge in Irish folk belief,
and was said to be useful when rescuing
a woman from fairy abduction!

**Crocosmia – *Crocosmia* (Irish:
fealeastram dearg)**

We see it everywhere in summer, but it is not
a native flower to our land – though there are
many who might beg to differ. A member of the
iris family, it is originally from the grasslands of
North and East Africa, but packs the punch of
a firework when you are out walking the land.

Flowers used in Carrowmore

- Astilbe – *Astilbe arendsii* (Irish: mórán)
- Crocosmia 'Lucifer' – *Crocosmia*
  (Irish: fealeastram dearg)
- Eucalyptus – *Eucalyptus* (Irish: eocalaip)
- Queen Anne's lace – *Ammi*
  majus (Irish: umbalaigh)
- Delphinium – *Delphinium*
  (Irish: sála fuiseoige)
- Lily of the valley – *Convallaria*
  majalis (Irish: lily an ghleann)
- Milkweed – *Asclepias* (Irish: buinneachan)
- Nigella – *Nigella damascena* (Irish: nigéal)
- Spiraea – *Filipendula ulmaria*
  (Irish: airgead luachra)
- Winter skimmia – *Skimmia* (Irish:
  unknown, trópaiceach)

Bláthanna: Irish Spaces in Flower

Earlsfort Place

Weekly flowers to make a workplace sing

St Stephen's Green, Dublin 2

'We spend 87% of our time inside buildings. How they are designed really affects how we feel, how we behave. Ultimately, design is a tool to enhance our humanity. It's a frame for life.'

Ilse Crawford

Extract from *A Frame for Life*

Monday mornings at our studio start in the early hours. The roller shutter comes up, the coffee machine gurgles, and everybody works at top speed to make flower arrangements for our clients that will last the coming week. This weekly flower work, an almost hidden part of every florist's business, is where we craft botanic marvels from organic materials and deliver each creation to their respective business, wherever that might be, so that they may welcome their own microcosm: the visitors, clients and people who work there. Our drivers know everyone at each reception space, and their visits are filled with chats of the weekend just gone. Every delivery is defined by the minute. By the time most people begin their working week, our crew have just moved on to their breakfast. Then they see what the rest of the flower-making day has to offer. The funny thing is that anyone outside our building won't have the opportunity to see or smell some of our most design-oriented displays, or know of the effort that goes into each and every welcome reception vase.

Studies show that flowers and plants in the workplace create a connection for the company team; they brighten the day, boost cognition, and act as a fruitful talking point. Findings by the Texas A&M University research team found that plants and flowers in an office space generate more creative and innovative thinking, ideas, and solutions. We love the privilege of being able to provide weekly flower displays that both represent each client's brand and act as a beautiful accessory in their given environment. All of our clients occupy spaces that have been designed with the intention of promoting business and creating a thriving culture for their people. We believe firmly in synchronicity, and that our flowers can help soften, subtly shape, and add finish to interior architecture; that their colour, form, texture, and volume follows, and elaborates upon, the traditional tenets of design.

> '**I think it's really important to design things with a kind of personality.'**
>
> **Marc Newson**

Flower engineering

As we make plenty of vase displays for clients every week, we feel like flower engineers. Starting with the vessel, we must ensure it has the right look, height, and colour. After that, the creative flower work begins. At times we have free rein; otherwise we must stick to particular conventions or colours – we must adjust according to whether a client prefers a naturalistic, wild, and woolly piece, or a contemporary, hothouse, tropical punkiness approach. Every florist has an obsession with detail and finish, and we are all influenced by visuals from other worlds – fashion, design, and daily life. We bind, twist, and weave foliage and flowers, bend twigs and grass, make knots of stems, making sure each vase is filled with creativity. The first caveat is that the displays are not to be fleeting beauties: they must last well for seven days. The other caveats, in no particular order, are that the vases must fit in the vans they are travelling in, the displays must be bound so that they are delivered in perfect condition, and the flower structures must properly dress the spaces in which they are placed.

And then we went to play

Our lovely client IPUT was just about to open a new building when we asked if we could take it over for a day. The reception space was filled with texture, lines, light and drama; it was yet to be furnished fully, but the pendant bulb cascades, the brass-lined marble, the gold, folded reception, and the shafts of daylight made it perfect for what we had intended. We imagined this welcome space as a place without financial or creative restraint, and decided to play with scale, because, given the reception's wonderful dimensions, we could.

Bláthanna: Irish Spaces in Flower

We found rounded concrete pots and made them into display vessels of delphinium. The summer date of our shoot allowed us some decadence; we were able to buy delphinium in all hues of blue and lavender. Their fluffy stems stood tall, over a metre in height, and we staggered each display to be part of a series, but simultaneously had each sit as a summer-day showcase in their own right. This flower, usually arranged in a more natural setting, came into its own on this occasion as a budding solo artist. The idea was to create a perfectly dramatic welcome, moving anyone who came through the revolving door to literally go over and smell the flowers.

And when we turned half-circle to the other side of the room, we wanted to show off the success of simplicity in flower design. We made a styled, sunny explosion using mokara and oncidium orchids in ambers, yellows and pinks, their stems fastened with sneaky, invisible fish gut (only the 20lb shark-bait type will do). The surface reflections, brass counter refractions, and leaning display made the entrance desk come to life in a new building that was ready and waiting to welcome its clientele.

Flowers

Delphinium – *Delphinium*
(Irish: sála fuiseoige)

This meadow flower is a favourite summer love of ours. Delphinium grows up to 120cm and can add drama to any large display. It is a member of the buttercup family and gets its name from the Greek for dolphin, because the flower petals reminded botanists of leaping dolphins. The rich colours of blue, lilac, and purple were used by Native Americans to dye their clothes and textiles. We use this tall, luxurious bloom to dress days of love, dramatic entrance spaces, and big bouquets. What is even lovelier is that, as a flower, delphinium represents positivity and protections against negativity, so that, no matter what, these flowery candles can only bring joy.

Flowers used in reception

Delphinium – *Delphinium*
(Irish: sála fuiseoige)

- Delphinium 'Centurion Sky Blue'
- Delphinium 'Dewy Boy'
- Delphinium 'Dewy Bstar'
- Delphinium 'Dewy Impress'
- Delphinium 'Night Queen'
- Delphinium 'Rose'

Orchids – *Orchidaceae* (Irish : Magairlín)

- Mokara orchid – x *Mokara aeridinae* (orange)
- Mokara orchid – x *Mokara aeridinae* (pink)
- Oncidium orchid – *Oncidium* (yellow)

Glendalough

A currach botanica

County Wicklow

Imagine a currach as a cover star, filling it with with native Irish flora foraged in the west, and then bringing it to one of Ireland's most iconic spots and floating it on a lake on an autumn, four-seasons-weather day. And then imagine Ultan and Ross, who owns said currach, following St Kevin's blackbird trick – holding out his hand as a nest after a blackbird laid an egg there – by hiding behind the flower boat for many hours so that we could create a magic flower moment for these pages. Our early autumn day in Glendalough, Co. Wicklow, began with chats with local walkers, all getting their fresh air before the flurry of tourist coaches arrived; from the sound of the visitors' speech, it seemed as though one nationality after another was arriving to stretch their legs on the short sandy beach. The rhythm of this routine was broken up by the beauty of an on-the-knee engagement proposal, which we were all privy to; this happened next to a girl floating in a light dress on dark water, as if she was Ophelia in *Hamlet*, for her husband's camera. It made for curious memories of Irish flowers in an Irish space.

The decision to create a currach botanica on Glendalough Upper Lake was made without us knowing how we would achieve any part of this floral story, but it was a story we wanted to tell nonetheless. We really had to convince the lovely folk of Wicklow National Park Office that we merely wished to float a boat on the water for the sake of flowers and not for boating. Everyone who worked in the park that day had a wonderful personal story to tell about their love for the lake and what it meant to them. These life stories added to our own memory of the lake and to the day yet ahead.

Luckily, we found Ross of Boyne Boats, who kindly brought his favourite currach, made with his own hands – the same one beloved by Jon Snow of *Game of Thrones* – all the way down to this glacial valley. Between finding and foraging much of what we wanted ourselves, and then asking our friend Ulli Rost to come up from Clare, we ended up bringing a van full of branches, birches, country lane stems, and lots of colour into the heritage park.

We layered the beautifully carved inside of the currach with covering so not even a single berry could leave its juice stains there that night. Almost as if constructing a pyre, hornbeam, larch, ash and beech were woven to form an interlocking base for us to then build our bounty of wildflower beauty upon.

The flora composition of the currach included ferns, deciduous branches, crocosmias, hydrangea, rosehips, viburnums, dahlias, delphiniums, acacias, heathers, berries, and more. This 20,000-hectare park has so many plant varieties – some from the Ice Age, most from natural migration to this country as attractive garden specimens or as seeds in cereal and food. Our Connemara boat could only hold so many, but we wanted to make the fall season colourways look marvellous while reflecting in the dark lake waters.

Although we started with blue skies that morning, shifts in weather were constant, as if intending to toy with dark and light. The mountain hills stretched down to the lake, visible through mist and clouds, sunlight and rain. The water constantly shifted from mossy greens and browns to a light sky blue; it moved from reflective calm, to waves like white horses, to ripples like those of the sea. A perfect cloud formation finally appeared, and our flower boat, mirrored in the water, began to appear.

And then, as we watched Sean taking shots of the boat, standing ladder-high above the surface, we pondered how the maidens made their way to see St Kevin of Glendalough, as he lived much of his 120 years in a tiny hermit hut on the steep hillside just above us. He had died 1,400 years ago, on 3 June 618. The poor man, tormented by lady suitors and followers, eventually had to abandon his ascetic life to form the monastic village and church that nearly every tourist and child in Ireland now visits.

Glendalough

Through intricate motions ran
Stream and gliding sun
And all my heart seemed gay:
Some stupid thing that I had done
Made my attention stray.
Repentance keeps my heart impure;
But what am I that dare
Fancy that I can
Better conduct myself or have more
Sense than a common man?
What motion of the sun or stream
Or eyelid shot the gleam
That pierced my body through?
What made me live like these that seem
Self-born, born anew?

W.B. Yeats
Extract from 'Stream and Sun at Glendalough'

The park flora in Glendalough

The currach

This National Park is a national treasure of 20,000 hectares. Not only is it home to diverse habitats such as mountains, bog, woodland, lakes, rivers and streams, but there are such dramatic views all around, if hiking up high. Such varied landscapes result in over eight hundred plant species – mostly native, some garden – who can thrive happily in their favourite part of the park. It is an unusual plant environment, as different communities of plants have evolved to coexist together in the mixed soil and terrain conditions. We felt blessed to be able to spend a full day there, arranging flowers in this beautiful native Irish boat.

The Irish currach has seen it all. Originally made of cured animal hides stretched over wooden slats, the boat was painted over with tar to seal where the skins met so that it floated perfectly. Contemporary methods involve using canvas and resin, but the delicate construction and carvings follow the traditional instructions.

Currachs have been around for thousands of years. St Brendan sailed in one for his sixth-century voyage to Newfoundland. They were used to transport building materials for Newgrange along the Boyne, and to trawl the Atlantic seaboard for new adventures. These amazing marine structures are going through a resurgence, too. There are active currach regattas all over Ireland, and Cork-based Meitheal Mara organise *An Rás Mór* (The Big Race), which brings traditional boats from all over the world to race the length of Cork Harbour up to the city. We will have to go to see it next time.

Flowers

Flowers used in currach

- Beech – *Fagus* (Irish: creann feá)
- Bilberry – *Vaccinium myrtillus* (Irish: fraochán)
- Birch – *Betula pendula* (Irish: beith)
- Bittersweet – *Celastrus scandens* (Irish: fuath oráiste)
- Burnet – *Sanguisorba* (Irish: lus an uille)
- Crocosmia 'Emily McKenzie' – *Crocosmia* (Irish: fealastram dearg)
- Dahlia 'Ivanetti' – *Dahlia* (Irish: dáilia)
- Erica 'Heather Pink' – *Calluna vulgaris* (Irish: fraoch mór)
- Honeysuckle 'Fuschia' – *Lonicera* (Irish: fiúise/deora dé)
- Hornbeam – *Carpinus betulus* (Irish: crainn slamhain)
- Hydrangea 'Elbtal Blue' – *Hydrangea macrophylla* (Irish: hiodrainsia)
- Larch – *Larix* (Irish: learóg)
- Delphinium – *Delphinium* (Irish: sála fuiseoige)
- Mimosa – *Acacia dealbata* (Irish: míomós)
- Red Hot Poker – *Kniphofia* (Irish : iarann dearg)
- Rosehip 'Corallo' (Irish: mogóir róis)
- Spindle – *Euonymus europaeus* (Irish: feoras)
- Guelder-rose – *Viburnum opulus* (Irish: caor chon)

Bláthanna: Irish Spaces in Flower

The Front Room

An indoor meadow reflects in resin

Dublin

'The most important thing in a solo concert is the first note I play, or the first four notes. If they have enough tension, the rest of the concert follows almost as a matter of course.'

Keith Jarrett

Ultan and I bought a house on what many told us was an unusual, hidden-away road, but we both knew the moment we saw it that this place would become our home. Whether it was the greater returns, the TARDIS-like feel, or that all the room measurements were uneven, this space struck us from the beginning and has become the cocoon for our family of four.

The front reception always fills with slanted light, because we live in a tall, Edwardian terraced house. In summertime, the blossom and wisteria leaves dapple the moving sunlight as it passes over the old floor and the chairs that constantly shift according to the play of the children who visit each day. Despite this, we think of this room's nature as still.

My work is primarily influenced by the scale, approach and aesthetic of the Irish landscape. I like to explore the cycle of life and decay, and the dichotomy of fragility and preservation. I am particularly interested in mankind's relationship with our surroundings, and expressing the nature of that interaction is central to my work. I like to work with unusual organic and locally found materials that tell intimate stories about the physical locality and expose man's interaction with the natural habitat.

Sasha Sykes

Having coveted a piece by Sasha Sykes, we met with her and collected flowers, foliage, and twigs to emulate the feeling of the reception room. Her work is influenced by our Irish landscape, and 'the dichotomy of fragility and preservation'. With midsummer flower heads of delphinium, cornflower, hydrangea, beech, and more, Sasha created a table in a shape that cut into the asymmetry of our navy velvet couch. The collected flowers were suspended in resin.

The Sasha Sykes table gave us the first four notes for our flower story. The navy couch sits along the wall behind this piece, reflecting in the table's resin surface. Inspired by the Irish summer garden suspended, layer by layer, in the surface – the sporadic placing of dusty blues, pinks, and greens; leaves and flowers heads – we decided to make the table more real than real. We made a meadow, using the couch as our stage and vessel.

A family of flower elements was chosen to come together as a fourth dimensional chorus to the carefully pressed selections in resin. The delicate wildflower style walked a line between a formal flower arrangement and a wild meadow as we convolutedly connected a theme between these two pieces of furniture art. Rhythms of dusty blue, pink, green, and burgundy made sense in this minimalist space. Kasia and I worked methodically, placing one floral ingredient at a time along the crevice where the wall met the seat. Having the time and space to make sure each stem stood at the right angle, their heads pointing correctly for the camera, showing off their colour and petals, was just heaven. As the sunlight increased with the approach of midday, the tabletop and tapestry of colours merged in mirrors of each other. Even better, it seemed as though our contrived juxtaposition was, surreally, meant to be.

And then we turned around. The concrete and iron fireplace, filled with sunlight and shadow, and the stark, white sculpture, crosscutting the grey, quickly led us to arrange as we did. Tree ferns and grass were made to explode, as if they had shuttled down the chimney on the downward sprint of a rollercoaster. The resulting shot is a luxurious burst of block-green colours with a grass knoll feel.

Our house is part of an original country house terrace built in 1904 when the Protestant gentry took to making homes away from their city homes across the Grand Canal. We are only the fourth owners of this space, but after chats with the neighbours, and visits from various musicians calling to our door, we discovered that Willy Hofmann lived here, along with hundreds of violins. A famous musician who once played with Seán Ó Riada in the Abbey Theatre, Mr Hofmann was unique in the annals of music-making in Ireland, and he passed a love and knowledge of fine instruments to many of his students while fixing any violin issue that arose. In an instance of life repeating itself, Mr Hofmann's music shop was originally on Lincoln Place, near our flower studio; it tickles us to think that he also cycled the same route to work every day, albeit in the name of a different creative pursuit.

Flowers

**Lady's mantle – *Alchemilla vulgaris*
(Irish: dearna mhuire)**

This Irish wildflower member of the rose
family Rosaecea was famed for its dew.
Medieval alchemists would collect it at dawn
and then turn base metals into gold!

**False buck's beard – *Astilbe
japonica* (Irish: astilbe)**

Beloved by butterflies and bees,
it means 'patience'.

Astrantia rose – *Astrantia* (Irish: scaibeas)

These pink pincushions are one of the
best perennials around, and add a rose-
tinted wildflower feel to any bunch.

**Chocolate cosmos – *Cosmos atrosanguineus*
(Irish: cosmas seacláid)**

A favourite flower; we love its velvety deep red
and brown petals, and its chocolate scent in a
daisy formulation. The word 'cosmos' in Greek
means 'orderly', 'beautiful', and 'ornamental'.

**Goat's beard – *Clematis
aristata* (Irish: gabhrán)**

This climbing shrub from the buttercup
family can be discovered all summer long
around our seaside country garden lanes.

**Quaking-grasses – *Briza media*
(Irish: fear gortach)**

A delicate and most attractive perennial
grass. Found throughout the country,
especially in the Burren region.

Flowers used on the couch

- Astrantia rose – *Astrantia* (Irish: scaibeas)
- Chocolate cosmos
- Cobra lily – *Darlingtonia californica*
- Delphinium – *Delphinium*
  (Irish: sála fuiseoige)
- False buck's beard – *Astilbe
  japonica* (Irish: astilbe)
- Garden cosmos – *Cosmos bipinnatus*
- Goat's beard – *Clematis
  aristata* (Irish: gabhrán)
- Lady's Mantle – *Alchemilla vulgaris*
  (Irish: dearna Mhuire)
- Nigella – *Nigella* (Irish: nigéal)
- Quaking-grasses – *Briza media*
  (Irish: fear gortach)
- Salvia nemorosa 'Caradonna'
  – *Salvia nemorosa*

Flowers used in the fireplace

- Silvergrass – *Miscanthus*
  (Irish: féar eilifinte)
- Panicum 'Green Mountain' – *Panicum
  virgatum* (Irish: féar panicum)

Bláthanna: Irish Spaces in Flower

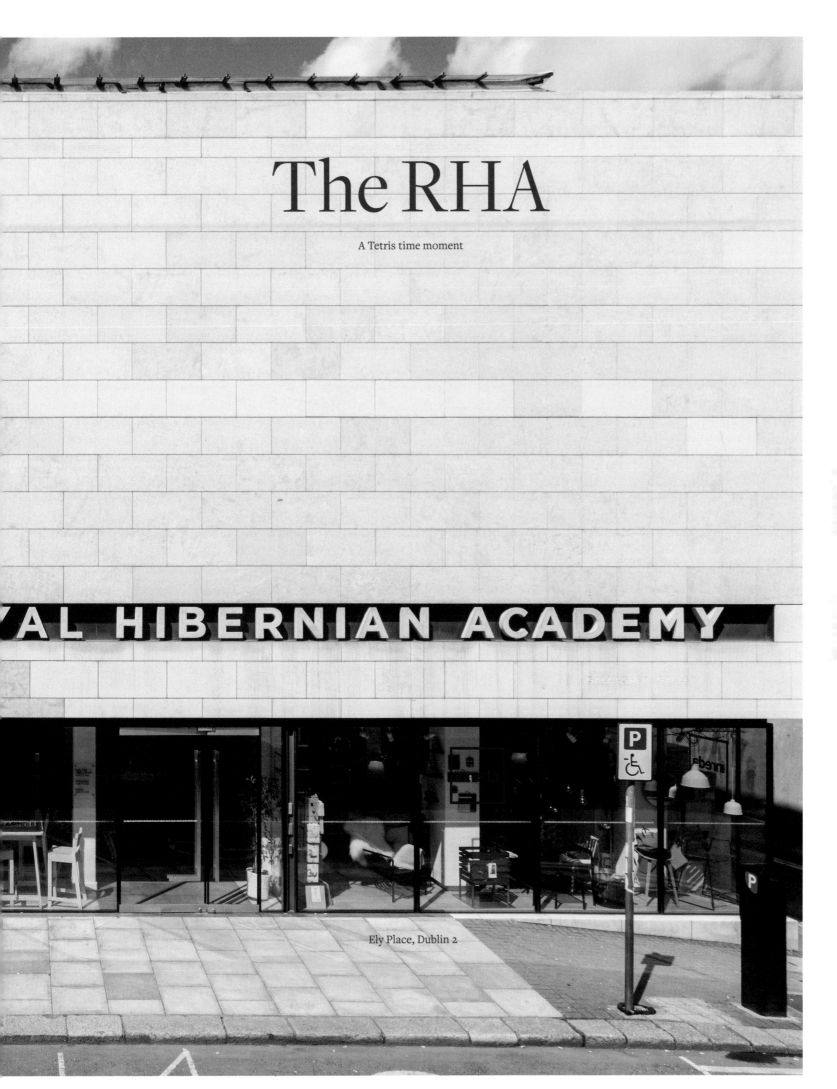

The RHA

A Tetris time moment

Ely Place, Dublin 2

'A gallery should be a blank canvas and whatever art is on or in it, it becomes that art.'

Patrick T. Murphy
RHA Director

The Royal Hibernian Academy gallery building has long been one of our favourites in Dublin. Not only does it lie on one of our busiest flower delivery routes, its facade makes our hearts flutter every time. This building, originally designed by Raymond McGrath RHA in the 1970s and reworked by Henry J. Lyons Architects in 2007, houses some of the most innovative visual art exhibitions in Ireland. The academy turns 200 in 2019, and has been directed by Patrick T. Murphy for over twenty of those years.

The gallery is the container for the art, and the art is what gives the articulation and excitement and what you need is a smart container but you don't need the container that itself is trying to be art.

Patrick T. Murphy
RHA Director

It is the stylish, quiet facade that stole our hearts. The simplicity of the polished, grey concrete and the modernist font of the 'Royal Hibernian Academy' signage, inset in front of a deep jade green, acts as a blank wall or canvas. In winter sunlight, the flushed glazing reflects the shadows of the opposite side of the street, whose Georgian chimney stacks make for an interesting juxtaposition. This contemporary building, first imagined in the seventies, is a definitive part of the Georgian street it sits in; the reflections also show how the building is a part of the street as much as the street is a part of the building. We were lucky to be able to borrow this canvas on a blue-sky Saturday in summer, using it to play a game of floral Tetris.

The intention was to allow our blooming tetrominoes (the geometric Tetris puzzle pieces) to play with the whole front of the building rather than have to shuffle the display into the smallest place possible. For such a minimal-looking shot, the preproduction behind it was extensive. We found adhesive pieces and toyed with their ability to stick and not leave residue marks, testing them on buildings near our studio on Pearse Street. Above all, we had to be mindful that the RHA facade was left in the pristine, fabulous condition in which we found it. Using large boards, we started to put together the botanically themed tetrominoes with big textures in mind so that each set would stand out against the grey.

We used hydrangea in blue and green, yellow chrysanthemums, purple lisianthus, and then we sprayed reindeer moss and gypsophilia in shades of red and orange so that the Tetris game colours were represented. All the stems were kept short, as we wanted to maintain a lightness of being with this installation. We took a chance by not feeding the flowers with water, as this might cause dripping onto the facade, and the heavier weight could cause the pieces to fall from a height. We knew the flowers would last for the duration of the shoot, which was all that was required. The idea was to have the red puzzle piece appear as if it was looking for a place to go.

Luckily that Saturday was a sunny day with a full, blue sky. This meant that there would be no shadows on our flower work. We hired a cherry picker to arrive at dawn. First, the adhesive elements were applied. Then, in a delicate pincer movement, and making use of our guidance, Ultan positioned the tetrominoes. The pieces had to be placed precisely so that they could properly act as accessories to the facade and represent the game they were bringing to life.

It took several hours to put this real-life floral Tetris together, involving lots of lifting and changing of heights. Sometimes our flower world can make for a workout – muscles can hurt, stress levels can rise – but it's always worth it when you get to step back and admire the achievement. On this occasion, when we made our way to the opposite side of the street and regarded our tetrominoes – filled with colour and joy on such a beautiful surface – each of us broke into a smile.

Bláthanna: Irish Spaces in Flower

Bláthanna: Irish Spaces in Flower

A little note on Tetris

Tetris turns thirty-five years old in 2019! Created in 1984 by computer programmer Alexey Pajitnov, it has become one of the most popular video games in the world.

Players must rotate, move, and drop tetrominoes that fall into the confined, rectangular matrix at increasing speeds. The idea is to clear as many lines as possible by completing horizontal rows of block without any spaces. It is all about strategy and speed.

A term has developed – 'The Tetris Effect' – which is used to describe the way people are inspired by the game to see tetrominoes in everyday situations. Because Tetris, like the real world, challenges people to make order out of chaos using a specific organisational system, the game's components translate easily into interpretations of life. Whether you're packing the trunk of your car, loading a dishwasher, or organising your shelves, you're likely thinking about how each object will fit together strategically so as to afford a minimum of empty space. This is the Tetris Effect!

Flowers

Flowers used at the RHA

- Dahlia 'Sunny Lady' – *Dahlia* (Irish: dáilia)
- Gypsophila 'White Victoria' – *Gypsophila paniculata*

- **Hydrangea 'Magical Royal Navy'** – *Hydrangea macrophylla* (Irish: hiodrainsia)
- Hydrangea 'Magical Summer Green'
- Lisianthus 'Alissa Purple' – *Eustoma grandiflorum* (Irish: coinnle corra)

- Reindeer Moss – *Cladonia rangiferina* (Irish: léicean réinfhia)

The Westbury Hotel

Studies in seasons

Balfe Street, Dublin 2

Appassionata have been our partners for twelve years at The Westbury and it is a relationship we highly value. Ruth Monahan and her team consistently exceed our expectations with beautifully scented, seasonal and luxurious floral displays. They are quite simply beautiful pieces of art and a famous talking point for our hotel guests, visitors and staff, who all stop, without fail, to admire and enjoy them.

Patrick King
CEO, *The Doyle Collection*

A hotel entrance is responsible for creating a mood. The lobby is where the guest first feels the welcome of where they are meeting, eating, or staying. This first moment should put the guest in a different place and set the tone for the rest of the time they spend there. The entrance of the Westbury Hotel leads you up a staircase to most of the hotel's spaces, and just before you check in – or visit the Gallery or Sidecar Bar – our flowers erupt on a central table in front of you.

There is a traditional relationship between a hotel and a florist – one that has become symbiotic. The hotel needs flowers that synchronise with their brand values and design. They need displays to reflect the interior's style and personality, dress the public space, set the tone in bedroom suites, and ensure that every event is filled with florals that suit the day or occasion. But a hotel is a microcosm of its own, its team working together to put the best foot forward for those visiting. The Westbury operates seamlessly in contending with a rollercoaster of people and events with an army of smiling staff, who we at Appassionata all know by name.

We are lucky enough to install new displays here every week. The marble table at the top of the stairs is so sizeable and prominent, it allows us to design large-scale arrangements that alter according to the season. It is an opportunity to create simple but artistic floral art that aims for impact each time it is seen.

Our team installs these displays early in the morning each Friday, just as the city centre comes to life. Some weeks we create a decadent dressing of brightness and colour, on others we make a subtle statement indebted to spring, or enjoy the understated elegance of presenting everything in white. Sometimes it is a reflection of whichever international rugby team Ireland is hoping to beat. Whatever the case, it is always on a grand scale, and the constant changing of seasons allows us to use different flowers, foliage, and shrubbery.

Much depends on the fancy we take as we sit in preproduction meetings the week before. We actually start the design by figuring out the vessels we will use. We then look at the flowers available to us and how we can arrange them in making a dramatic yet understated centrepiece. We then wait until opening the studio early on a Thursday morning. If our selection has arrived perfectly in stature, colour and size, we move ahead with the plan. If not, the improvisation is real and we rework and rely on inspiration.

We became flamboyant on four occasions this year when filling this fabulous marble table with odes to each season. Given the great budget we were afforded, we had a marvellous opportunity to experiment.

Autumn

Autumn is a favourite time for any florist. There are berries and shrubs to forage, colours are deep, textures have volume, and we can have a lot of fun. We filled the one-metre-high chimney vases and the eighty-centimetre cylinders with clear water and let the light refraction from the chandeliers above begin. Giant tangles of magnolia branches, just about bursting with their first buds, made a foraged forest wall; these leaned over berries, terracotta-orange 'bittersweet' branches, and red chilli fruit trees. We gathered every pumpkin and gourd we could find when they came back from their contract visits that Halloween week, and, because we could, we piled them high, fruit market style. Colours of creamy white, orange, and green mixed with the textures of wrinkled, lined, spotted skins. In the pile-up, the pumpkins were further warped by the miniscus and water.

Winter

There is an art in preparing amaryllis to be displayed for an entire week. These flowers look so unassuming as they arrive, lying in beds of foam under cardboard lids. However, we have to create grids on top of our flower buckets so that each individual flower is allowed to bloom. Stamens are removed with rapid pinches. Depending on the winter temperature, the heads burst into bloom within three to five days, stunning guests with petal arrays the size of an outstretched hand.

We wanted to create some winter glamour to counteract a grey week in January. Clear glass vessels were chosen, cylindrical, staggered in size, with curved rectangles of crystal. Leaning the back-wall stems is a deft art, as the angle must work with the opening of the vessel top. The idea was that these heroes would be the ones to catch the eye of anyone climbing the stairs to check in. We played with rubies, reds, and whites, which shouldn't work together on the colour wheel, but did in this case, as each is intrinsic to the amaryllis blends. By simply hiding our binding with an aspidistra leaf in every vase and letting the water stay below where the flowers were tied, the tall, green stems and the bursting balloons of flowers made for an explosive lightness of amaryllis.

Spring

Green flowers are often misunderstood; some clients will send them back, thinking we have only given them leaves. But when we are able to make giant snowballs of bouncing guelder-rose that act like a large cloud sitting above the most elegant of stems, we have almost everything we need to fend against the misconception. These long, statuesque stems can lean out of vases in an elegant fashion, or can stand tall to create a dramatic look. To this display we added hellebores, so beloved in our winter gardens, which have a gorgeous green hue that makes for a wilder feel. And then, just to balance the back wall of lime, we added in heavenly hortensia, just starting their spring season; they provided a light-green tone.

Summer

This table is all about everyone's favourite summer flowers – we wanted to make a blue-sky moment. A wet, dark winter meant that tall, gnarly stems of Irish cherry blossom, with their bouncing balls of candyfloss pink, arrived in summer instead. Kasia has a friendly neighbour who let us 'borrow' these branches, so reminiscent of my own granny's beloved blossom tree, and they were perfect. Big blue clouds of hydrangea held high in front of the cherry blossom, and then coral peonies bloomed and opened out their petals perfectly like large scoops of ice-cream; we simply put them in a sumptuous dome. Some Irish sweet pea, grown in Meath, was added to this set piece. The scent and the seamless integration of May flowers was the finishing touch in this early summer styling.

Flowers

Flowers used in autumn display

- Bittersweet – *Celastrus scandens*
  (Irish: fuath dubh)
- Magnolia – *Magnolia grandiflora*
  (Irish: magnóilia)
- Pumpkins – *Cucurbita* (Irish: puimciní)

Flowers used in winter display

    Amaryllis – *Hippeastrum* (Irish: amaryllis)
- Amaryllis 'Ambiance' – *Hippeastrum*
- Amaryllis 'Reve'
- Amaryllis 'Showmaster'
- Amaryllis 'Spider Tarantula'

Flowers used in spring display

- Guelder-rose – *Viburnum*
  opulus (Irish: caor chon)
- Green-flowered helleborine – *Epipactis*
  phyllanthes (Irish: cuaichín glas)
- Hydrangea 'Elbtal' – *Hydrangea macrophylla*

Flowers used in summer display

- Sweet pea 'Dark Flamingo' –
  Lathryus (Irish: pis chumhra)
- Sweet pea 'Misty Rose Red'
- Sweet pea 'Sunset Lavender'
- Sweet pea 'Sunset Mauve'
- Sweet pea 'Sunset Rose'
- Sweet pea 'Neon Salmon'
- Peony 'Coral Charm' – *Paeonia*
  lactiflora (Irish: piaine)
- Peony 'La Reine Hortense'
- Peony 'Flame'
- Pink cherry blossom – *Prunus serrulate*
  (Irish: bláth an chrainn silíní)

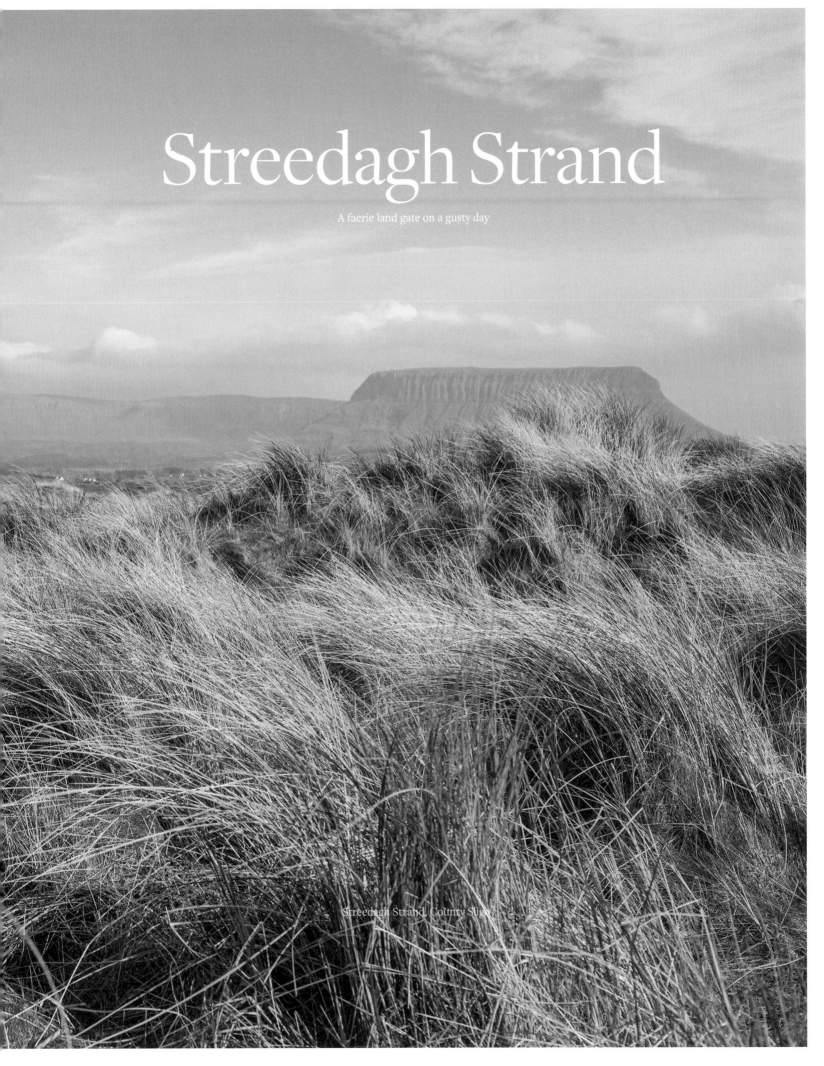

Streedagh Strand

A faerie land gate on a gusty day

Streedagh Strand, County Sligo

'Sligo is, indeed, a great place for fairy pillaging of this kind. In the side of Ben Bulben is a white square in the limestone. It is said to be the door of fairyland. There is no more inaccessible place in existence than this white square door; no human foot has ever gone near it, not even the mountain goats can browse the saxifrage beside its mysterious whiteness. Tradition says that it swings open at nightfall and lets pour through an unearthly troop of hurrying spirits. To those gifted to hear their voices the air will be full at such a moment with a sound like whistling.'

W.B. Yeats
Extract from 'Irish Fairies'

Let's build a moon-gate-style doorway to Benbulben as an ode to the fairies and to the Fianna, we said. Not only is this glacial plateau a defining piece of Sligo's landscape, but traditionally it was believed that it is the only place in Ireland where fairies are visible to mortals. It was believed, and still is, that whenever the door, which is the white patch on a bare hollow on the north face of the mountain, opens, there will be good weather for a week. And it is in the shadow of this mountain that W.B. Yeats is buried, too.

This tabletop mountain also provides a setting for the mythological stories of the Fianna; Fionn MacCumhaill and his gang loved hunting in its shadow. Fionn first met his bewitched wife Sadhbh here, but only spent seven years with her before she was turned into a deer. In a brighter narrative, it is on the top of the mountain that he found his son Oisín, who then turned out to be a famous member of the Fianna. There is also the saga of Diarmuid and Gráinne, who famously lived in a cave on the mountain, hiding from the wrath of Fionn after the two eloped; after sixteen years, poor Diarmuid was killed by Fionn masquerading as a boar and Gráinne soon followed from grief over his death, resulting in sadness for all. We have always loved reading the legends, especially *Tóraíocht Dhiarmada agus Ghráinne*, and wanted to draw from their narratives in our work.

So we decided on the colour pink, and that the delicate asparagus fern – although it's actually a tropical climber – would provide a definitive contrast to the marram grass on which the gate would stand. Although we did forget about how the Atlantic Ocean and beach dunes are always accompanied by strong winds. With Edmundo at the helm in the studio, we fashioned a circle of wire, asparagus fern, and a florist fastening wire, which we could never work without. After taking the moon gate out of our van, the three of us shuffled it along the lagoon behind Streedagh Beach. Larks warbled in the dunes, laughing at our red faces as we stumbled over humps and bumps where the grass had grown to protect the sand hills that surrounded.

Our skin was being punctured by dune grass and burning wind, but our wished-for panorama came to us after Ultan fashioned supports and tripwires to make the floral structure stand. When we let go, it stood, fern fronds waving, marram grass gusting, Benbulben showing off its glacial, creviced glory in the background. It was a cause for celebration.

Fuelled by our first successful outdoor moon gate and the beautiful blue sky, we brought the piece along to mark where the beach meets the dunes, and the walks begin. We held it as if in a tug of war so that this circle of ferns could stand proudly before Streedagh Strand. And then we let the moon gate rest amidst the dunes, where it seemed to relish its surrounds, looking perfectly at home in bent grass with primroses popping up as a surprise. The marram and asparagus moved perfectly in rhythm with the movements of the wind.

A favourite beach is a bonding subject for all three of us, whether it's in south Mayo or north Sligo. Streedagh in north Sligo is a curving spit of sand that stretches from Streedagh Point to Connor's Island; it is filled with history. The monastic island of Inishmurray was visible as the tide ran out, leaving the sand glistening, reflecting the light of the late afternoon sky. We carried our beloved fairy moon gate to the shore, letting it rest amongst the sandworm spaghetti and rippling waves; its rose-filled fern fluttered and flew.

The moon gate started to look like a large *Aurelia aurita* jellyfish, non-stingers who usually arrive in August on the Streedagh shore. It began to melt and morph, becoming part of the sandscape. We couldn't be sure it didn't feel an affinity with the many fossils of ancient coral-coloured sea limestone appearing in the grains.

As it floated in a few inches of water, we were reminded of the twelve hundred Spanish Armada soldiers who met their end in shipwrecks along the beach in 1588. The ships were called *La Lavia, La Juliana* and the *Santa Maria de Visón*. The wrecks lie beneath the sands, but many items, including cannon and other artefacts, have been recovered and are under conservation. Captain Francesco de Cuéllar managed to survive both the shipwreck and the attack. His diary entries, detailing the story of his escape back to Spain via Antrim and Scotland, are a fascinating read.

Once the sun started to set, we carried our moon gate back to the van, catching loose, pink fronds that whirled in the wind. We settled into our seats, feeling the glow of Streedagh Strand in our hearts; our cheeks matched the pink of the fern of fairies. We thanked them for all they gave.

Flowers

Flowers used in moon gate

Common asparagus fern/lace fern – *Asparagus setaceus* (Irish: raithneach asparagais)

Restaurant Patrick Guilbaud

An experiential orchestra we love

Merrion Street, Dublin 2

'Every detail matters to us because it adds something more to the customer experience. Fine dining is not just about food, it's the whole package – the surroundings, the service and the ambience. All the customer should have to do is enjoy the experience as a whole, without being able to exactly pinpoint why. It's seamless. They should never be aware of the machinations behind the scenes.'

Stéphane Robin

Extract from *Restaurant Patrick Guilbaud: The First Thirty Years*

It is no secret in our studio that our favourite client meetings are those with Stéphane Robin in Restaurant Patrick Guilbaud. When he himself makes you a coffee, and the most beautifully set tray of treats arrives, with each detail more divine than the last, be it the spoons, the cups, or the textures, we wish that we could stay chatting about food, flowers, and business for the rest of the day. We have been bringing our flowers to this magical two-Michelin-starred restaurant every Tuesday morning for eleven years. We still feel a thrill and excitement as we watch the team there set tables for lunch: an orchestra so well conducted that a part of you wishes you could work there for a while. When chatting with Stéphane, it is clear that he focuses on details and personal touches as much as anything else, from the tablecloths to the glassware, to the flowers we supply. It is so important to him and his team that his guests absorb all the meaningful small touches, making their two-Michelin-starred experience magical.

Behind the black, gloss-painted door, guests are welcomed into an unusual rose-tint-walled hall where coats are taken and smiling faces beckon you to the beautiful Spyglass Bar. This Zelouf & Bell rounded masterpiece of marquetry sits on a sparkling carpet, surrounded by seating expectant of the guests' arrival. We wanted to make a display inspired by this master-crafted piece, resplendent in the manner of the spring season.

A wildscape piece, asymmetrical and almost pompous in comparison to the subtle sophistication of the space, was imagined. An all-white affair, reminiscent of what might feature at a Jay Gatsby party. Delphinium, prunus, peonies, ranunculus, and hellebores were arranged in an organic, tiered tangle, and then jasmine plants were added for decadence, twirling and throwing down their lengths of white scent. The rounded wall piece, the curvature of the countertop, the moulded, bronzed pot – it all provided a circular movement which was literally interrupted by our informally formal explosion of blooms.

To dress a two-Michelin-starred restaurant table is a precise affair. As guests walk down the steps into the rose-gold, gilded, barrel-vault-ceilinged dining room, their attention is first grabbed by the sheer scale of the space, the volume of light and bright. The 1986 Sean Scully Abala piece dominates the back wall; we once removed it for a Brown Thomas catwalk in order to make a giant wall of flowers. But it is when sitting down that the true craft of setting a table can be admired: cutlery and glassware are positioned exactly on starched, heather-grey tablecloths, and, arranged by ourselves, dusky pink dried urchins sit beside a fluffy pink bud vase. Our most beloved addition to this table beautification is the individually sized Orla De Brí sculptures sitting pretty, as if each particular dining table is their home of rest.

Inspired by the Abala tones, we decided to create more formal pieces with which to dress the tables, as if Sean Scully had dictated the mood board himself. Humbled by the majesty of the Michelin-level table setting, we chose the delicate, paper-layered ranunculus – a domed kaleidoscope of white, orange, red, yellow, Guilbaud-pink and burgundy – and placed them in metallic gold vessels. The scale of this room meant that even by using one hundred flower stems for each table centre, they did nothing to overpower the setting. Yet their colour pops resonated, and, in true Restaurant Patrick Guilbaud style, each table looked dressed for the ritual of high-end dining.

The private dining room is situated just beside the Spyglass Bar. It is a space where tables transform to fit the occasion. It could be fit with a long dining table that seats ten on either side, or it might just as easily fit a small, square table for four. It could be occupied by high drinks tables or set for a wedding party. We filled the long table's large centre with a march of ranunculus, one stepping after the other, to celebrate whatever occasion was fulfilled with the arrival of the next guests.

Flowers

Flowers used in Spyglass Bar

- White astilbe japonica 'Washington' – *Astilbe japonica* (Irish: astilbe)
- White broom – *Cytisus scoparius* (Irish: giolcach shléibhe)
- White delphinium 'El Dewi Siberia' – *Delphinium grandiflorum* (Irish: deilfiniam)
- White delphinium 'Volkerfried'
- White cherry blossom – *Prunus* (Irish: bláth an chrainn silíní)
- White hellebore – *Helleborus orientalis* (Irish: eileabar bán)

- White hydrangea – *Hydrangea macrophylla* (Irish: hiodrainsia)
- White lilac – *Syringa vulgaris* (Irish: líológ)
- White peony 'Duchesse de Nemour' – *Paeonia* (Irish: piaine)

Flowers used in restaurant

Ranunculus 'Cloni Folkers' – *Ranunculus asiaticus* (Irish: fearbán)
- Ranunculus 'Cloni Mandarino'
- Ranunculus 'Cloni Venere'
- Ranunculus 'Super Alaska'

Flowers used in private dining room

- Ranunculus 'Cloni Folkers'
- Ranunculus 'Cloni Mandarino'
- Ranunculus 'Cloni Venere'
- Ranunculus 'Super Alaska'

Bláthanna: Irish Spaces in Flower

Huntington

A daydream swing

Clonegal, County Carlow

'In a Wonderland they lie,
Dreaming as the days go by,
Dreaming as the summers die:
Ever drifting down the stream –
Lingering in the golden gleam –
Life, what is it but a dream?'

Lewis Carroll
Extract from 'A Boat Beneath a Sunny Sky'

The decision to make a kaleidoscopic swing of gypsophila amidst an arboricultural curiosity in a garden wonderland was one that made for a day of joy. We dabbled with a daydream by hanging a surreal, colourful structure from a natural yew, a cathedral of growth. The idea was to create an imaginary place in a space that already exists, and the grounds of Huntington Castle in Clonegal, Co. Carlow, provided us with a playground in which to do so.

Gypsophila paniculate, or 'baby's breath' as most brides would call it, is a hardy, herbaceous perennial plant. It is a flower that is definitely celebrating its retour: haute couture fashion shows, events, and days of love are all allowing the tiny white blossom buds back into a circle of taste. We florists love to make it wisp along century-old wooden flooring, circle around moon gates, garland it on heads and shoulders, and make mountains and molehills for fashionable photographic moments in time.

Inspired by the UK photographer Cecil Beaton's 'playful eye', we decided to buy neon rainbow paint sprays in a skateboard shop in town. We wanted to perpetuate the idea of a swing of more unusual beauty. We felt that Irish yew – one of the 'noble four' in Irish tree history, usually tarred with a depressed status – deserved some joy and happiness for an afternoon. Armed with graffiti paint and gypsophila, we made a makeshift swing structure in the studio and prepped it to hang amidst the branches in front of a castle of many histories, some of which one might already know without realising the location.

We were followed to the six-hundred-year-old yew walk by a brood of curious hens and a resplendent peacock called Percy, all of whom perhaps thought we would bring them somewhere new. We lugged our large swing of dreams until we made it to the very end of the 120-metre-long path; an interlacing of branches stretched outwards from each yew trunk and made us feel that we had stepped into a mystical tunnel. But there was an authentic beauty here, a stillness that surrounded; we could feel the positive spirit of the earth and surrounds as we stepped up on ladders to steady the swing in the whispering winds. The trees seemed to envelop the enormous swing we thought we had made, making it appear smaller in stature than what it really was. We had to make our right-angled 'C' fluffy as a cloud and so stuffed it with colour, baby's breath, and intention. Sunlight and shadows played together in the breeze, and the hues faded up and down in tone, depending on the clouds. The union of a modern-day flower's flamboyance and an ancient canopy of knitted yew trees created a fantastical story which made everyone who saw it that day smile.

Histories of the Irish yew
Irish yew – *Taxus baccata* 'fastigiata' (Irish: Iúr)

In ancient Ireland, the yew is considered part of the big four, along with ash, oak and hazel. Niall Mac Coitir notes in *Ireland's Trees*, 'All four have myths involving them as a protector or marker of important places in a sacred and social sense, while also having much folklore attached to them.' As one of the 'nobles of the wood', the yew had laws governing its use and there were fines for damaging or cutting them down without permission in ancient *Bretha Comaithchesa* ('Laws of the Neighbourhood').

Due to their long life expectancy, yews were planted at sacred sites and marked the boundaries of churches and graveyards; they were also made into croziers and shrines for books. Mac Coitir notes that in the poem 'Battle of Gabhair', which describes the graves of the Fianna, there is mention of 'beautiful Ireland of the yew trees'. However, due to its toxic nature and regular planting in graveyards, this native evergreen became associated with death and eternity. It is usually planted and celebrated at Samhain, our native feast of the dead and celebration of approaching winter, going back to pagan times.

I love the stillness of the wood:
I love the music of the rill:
I love to couch in pensive mod
Upon some silent hill.
Scarce heard, beneath yon arching trees,
The silver-crested ripples pass;
and, like a mimic brook, the breeze
Whispers among the grass.
Here from the world I win release,
Nor scorn of men, nor footstep rude,
Break into mar the holy peace
Of this great solitude.

Lewis Carroll
Extract from 'Solitude'

When poison is a healer

Although Irish yew is poisonous to most animals, deer love to chew the branches when they can. Also, the bark of these ancient trees contains anti-cancer compounds from which Taxol, used in chemotherapy to halt production of cancer cells, is derived. Hanging a rainbow-bright swing of gypsophila on the yew tree added extra healing kudos, as the flower has healing properties and is used in cures for leukaemia. In a symbiotic fashion, these tiny flowers are deer-resistant too – who knew there was so much in common between gypsophila and yew.

Welcome to Huntington Castle

In the case of Huntington Castle, one senses that those feet may be in a state of eternal, ethereal tap-dancing. The sumptuous Jacobean castle is located in a valley criss-crossed by rivers and encircled by hills with the stunning violet slopes of Mount Leinster rising highest of all. The avenue begins in the handsome village of Clonegal, an ancient settlement whose Irish name 'Cluain na nGall' translates as 'Meadow of the Foreigners'. Quite who the foreigners were is anybody's guess. Perhaps they were the fairies for whom a dolmen known as the Tomb of Laba na Sighe was erected some 3,000 years ago. In the thirteenth century, the peaceful riverside setting attracted Franciscan monks from afar who established a priory. The monks planted a yew tree walk of 120 trees, beneath whose evergreen and interlocking branches one can merrily stroll today. But be careful, because one might stumble into the vaporous form of one of these very same monks. Unsurprisingly to anyone who has visited Huntington, this is a demesne with a high quota of ghosts.

Turtle Bunbury

The site of Huntington Castle was originally occupied by a monastery. The yews were planted on Halloween some six hundred years ago to create an outdoor cloister: an ambulatory covered passage for the monks.

Originally owned by the Esmonde family, who planted the formal gardens and lime-tree-lined avenue, it is now the home of the Durdin-Robertson family, and is run by Alex and Clare, who we were delighted to meet. Huntington was used as the location for Stanley Kubrick's *Barry Lyndon* and, in true yew-associative fashion, it is also the home of the Fellowship of Isis.

Given how these trees have always been planted close to a spiritual home, it is fitting that the fellowship is in such proximity to the yew walk. The tree's associations also align it with the goddess of the land, so we found it fascinating to discover that Huntington is home to a spiritual platform which celebrates the importance of female goddesses – and Isis, the mother of all, in particular. This fellowship was formed in the seventies by Olivia, Pamela and Lawrence Durdin-Robertson, and now has a membership of over twenty-five thousand people, some of whom gather there four times a year for an Isis festival. Further otherworldly links include the falling of a meteorite onto the front avenue, where it glowed for two years.

Bláthanna: Irish Spaces in Flower

Flowers

Baby's breath – *Gypsophila paniculata*

This flower is loved or hated, depending on who we talk to. It is actually one of the most widely used flowers worldwide, and is available in white or pink. A descendant of the carnation family, the tiny white blossom buds signify everlasting love, freedom, and innocence. The name comes from the Greek *gypsos,* the gypsum soil it loves to grow in, and *philios,* which means 'loving'. The common name 'baby's breath' derives from its innocent meaning. We love to use it in big quantities to make clouds, swings, and pretty things, but you will never see us combine it with red roses for sale on the street!

Bláthanna: Irish Spaces in Flower

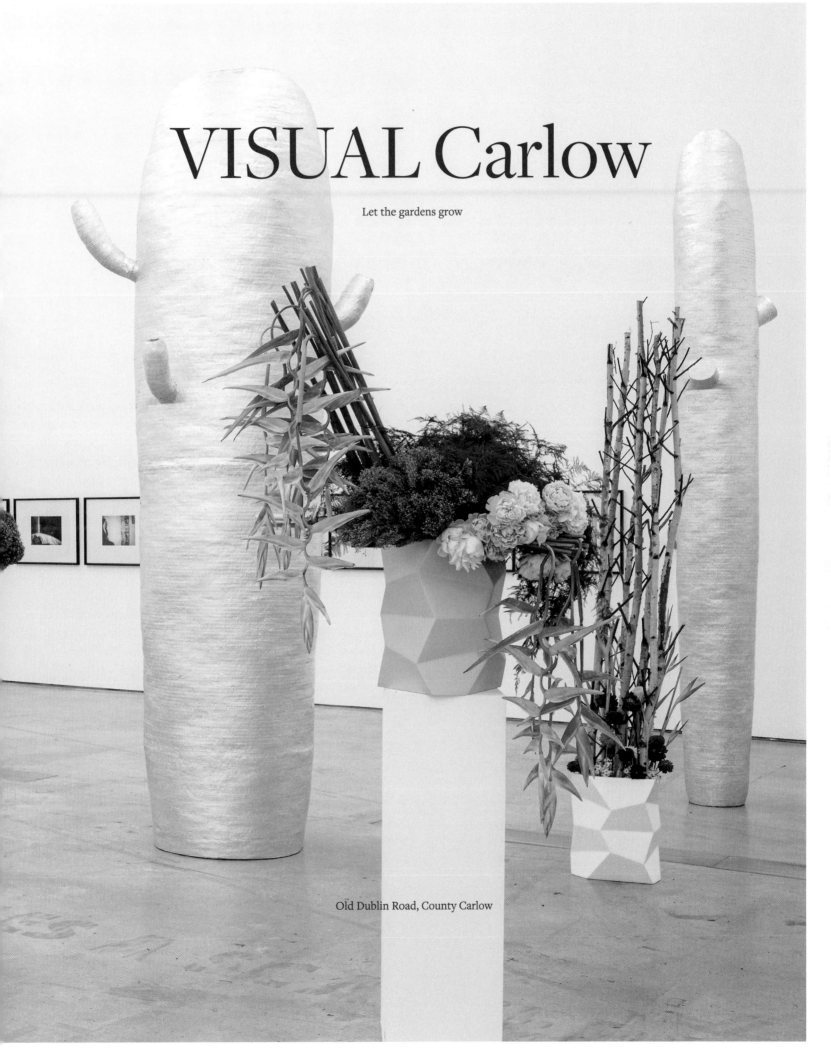

VISUAL Carlow

Let the gardens grow

Old Dublin Road, County Carlow

As florists we are so aware of the luck we have in life, because we get to work with beautiful things. However, the sense of joy we get as each season brings new flowers as fruit comes with a strong sense of responsibility. Due to global warming and advancements in flower growth, our new normal is that we can access flowers throughout the year that used to be seasonal. Delphiniums in December, garden roses all year round, hydrangea from south of the equator, and more. Nevertheless, we are almost completely dependent on importing flowers through Holland to maintain a steady stream of ingredients for our business.

As we wrote this series of short flower stories, the flower market in Smithfield, Dublin, closed forever. We, as a country, have lost a fresh flower community that existed for two centuries.

Although we strive to use as many Irish-grown ingredients as possible, we need more and more of them. We can access the most amazing foliage, twigs, berries, lichen, moss, and pine from Clare, Kerry, and Waterford, and from the wonderful growers we know and love. There is nothing better than Killowen-grown daffodils arriving in the door, their fragrance filling our regulars with glee. Then comes summer. We have a flower friend who grows sweet pea for us, and we love to have peonies, dahlias, and garden roses dropped in for special wedding days. But apart from that, we get stuck, and everything has to arrive by ferry over the Irish Sea. We make use of a mix of native flowers and flowers from all over the world. What is important to note is that we floristas insist that any bloom we use must be from a supplier who is bound to the Floriculture Sustainability Initiative for 2020. Their objective reads:

> **The Floriculture Sustainability Initiative was initiated in 2012 by 25 stakeholders in the floriculture sector, the founding members of FSI. They share the goal of finding more sustainable solutions for farmers, for the environment, and for the future of the sector, and set themselves the ambition to have 90% flowers and plants responsibly produced and traded by 2020.**

Our collective consciousness about how global warming is changing our planet is, thankfully, becoming stronger. Studies by the US National Oceanic and Atmospheric Administration show how warmer winters mean that different plants and flowers are now able to grow farther north. Our native botanical environments are changing, and will change more. This means that our landscape will change in appearance and feel as more Mediterranean flora begins to grow naturally here in our countryside.

If we look at our own island, the need to grow flowers and foliage in a biodiverse environment should be written in neon lights for all to see. This is especially crucial given the need to rebuild our bee population. Dr Úna Fitzpatrick, co-founder and Project Coordinator of the All-Ireland Pollinator Plan, and Senior Ecologist with the National Biodiversity Data Centre, has the following to say on this dire need:

One third of our 98 wild bee species are threatened with extinction from the island and our common bumblebee species have experienced a 14.2% decline in abundance in the last five years. Rare species are disappearing through habitat loss, and our common species are struggling because there simply isn't enough food for them across our landscape. Pollinators are in enormous difficulties, but we don't have to accept that. We can change their fate. It's not about feeding tired bees a spoonful of sugar water. Pollinators need us to move away from seeing the landscape as purely a human space that should be kept neat and tidy. It's not about letting things go wild, but we do need to let nature back in or we risk losing its vital free services. It's about retaining healthy hedgerows on farms and allowing them to flower; not using herbicides so freely to tidy up our public spaces;

planting more native flowering trees; not cutting grass so often – so that pollen-rich Dandelion and Clover can grow and provide food, and planting pollen and nectar-rich flowers in our parks and gardens.

More native flowers in our landscape means more pollinators and other insects. More flowers mean more fruits and seeds, and therefore more birds and mammals. More flowers also mean a more distinct, more colourful, and more attractive environment for us to live in, and for visitors to experience. In taking simple actions to help bees, we gain so much more!

We decided to create a floral story, or allegory, in VISUAL Carlow to comment on global warming and how biodiversity in the growing world of flowers could work; how this could benefit bees, butterflies, humans, and our souls.

VISUAL Carlow is not just one of our island's leading contemporary art spaces, with four galleries and an amazing performance space; its mission is to enrich, inspire, and improve the everyday through art. The gallery also has a focus on their grounds being as full of biodiversity as possible, and the team there is very involved in ensuring that its Carlow community is also integrated. The thoughtful architectural design of the building means that the Main Gallery is lit by natural light all day and the Link Gallery looks out on to a pond of curious fish and beautiful bulrushes, as if a lake on a headland.

The Main Gallery

Link Gallery

Each of the Main Gallery's five flower installations stands alone in their illustration of the future of floristry, and collectively they combine to imagine how our landscape might appear – how our flowers might grow side by side – as the earth warms up. Lots of the flowers we chose suit the current 'Farmland Guidelines', included in the All-Ireland Pollinator Plan and described as evidence-based actions that make farmland more pollinator friendly.

The guidelines are as follows:

1. Maintain native flowering hedgerows.
2. Allow wildflowers to grow around the farm.
3. Provide nesting places for wild bees.
4. Minimise artificial fertiliser use.
5. Reduce pesticide inputs.

The gallery text for the exhibition in VISUAL read, 'This year's open call invited artists to submit work that comments on the trials of our post-truth world and the potential of collective energy using Prince lyrics as a call to action. Time, labour, love, loss, coping mechanisms, and space for imagining for the future.' We felt that this exhibition's mantra was serendipitous in having a similar approach to the way we ourselves had thought of the flower installations. We were also fortunate to have Daphne Wright's *Where do Broken Hearts Go* – stark, layered, foil-strip, oversized cacti – as a dramatic background to contrast with our flowers.

Stark, sustainable fibreglass in cobalt-blue, rose-pink, and white were placed on white plinths. We tried to imagine what flower displays might look like in the future as more and more tropical varieties grow in Northern Hemisphere climes. And a word of warning: none of these combinations look like they could work in flower school, but somehow, in the VISUAL environs, we believed they did.

And then we went to the Link Gallery, where on a muzzy grey summer's day we could sit in a space structure specially designed by Tom Watt and Tadhg McSweeney and make imagined future meadows that could help bring back the bees.

Terrazzo, rainbow-bright troughs were stacked, Jenga-style, in the centre of the space to catch the natural light. We wanted everyone to see that by planting pollinator pieces in containers in even the smallest outdoor space it would help the environment, because not everyone has a garden or a field to play with. Inspired by environmental artist Herman de Vries and his comment, 'Humanity will fade, nature will prevail', we wanted to try and show what the reality of a globally warmed wild pollinator meadow or planter might look like.

Angelica gigas, poppies, dahlias, endangered meadow barley, giant alliums. Yes, these are all Irish countryside familiars, but then we popped in punky gloriosa and sassy heliconia as happy garden companions. The latter two, native to Central and South America, could easily grow here if winter keeps warming up. What is likely the essential essence of this piece is that, yes, our flower-growing possibilities in Ireland will expand and yes, there could be more tropical stems. However, by allowing our native flowering varieties to exist alongside these flowers that come about through climate change, we will help our biodiverse environment. And then, if all farmers, growers, and gardeners stand together as a concerted team, we could create the best orchestra for playing the best environmental tune.

Bláthanna: Irish Spaces in Flower

The stage

We were just about to go when we stood on the stage in the almost hidden-away VISUAL performance space. As it was our last shoot for this book, we thought it pertinent to celebrate the joy of all that we did. This part of our VISUAL floral story is an explosion of blooming joy. The abundance, the colour, the combinations of fresh, dry plants, native and tropical, summed up our reality in being able to disco-dance through seasons, days, and weeks in our floral, technicolour world. Our addiction to making, creating, and working with flowers knows no bounds, and no matter how tired we might feel after a busy day, there is always that joy when the roller shutter goes up and we see the next day ahead in flower form.

'Dearly beloved,
We are gathered here today
To get through this thing called life.'

Prince

Extract from 'Let's Go Crazy'

Flowers

Flowers used in Main Gallery

Pink, Medium
- Asparagus fern – *Asparagus aethiopicus* (Irish: raithneach asparagais)
- Dried Broom – *Cytisus scoparius* (Irish: giolcach shléibhe)
- Heliconia 'Sexy Pink' – *Heliconia chartacea* x *platystachys*
- Peony 'Sarah Bernhardt' – *Paeonia* (Irish: piaine)

Pink, Small
- Allium 'Ambassador' – *Allium*
- Asparagus fern – *Asparagus aethiopicus* (Irish: raithneach asparagais)
- Heleconia 'Prince of Darkness' – *Heleconia caribaea*
- Phalaenopsis orchid 'Magic Art' – *Phalaenopsis*
- Poppy – *Papaver rhoeas* (Irish: cailleach dhearg)

Blue, Small
- Agave leaves – *Agave americana*
- French ruscus (bleached) – *Ruscus*
- Gloriosa rothschild – *Gloriosa superba* (Irish: glóir lile)
- Hosta 'Big Daddy' – *Hosta*
- Korean angelica – *Angelica gigas* (Irish: allfheabhrán)
- Leucospermum 'Tango' – *Leucospermum*
- Nutans (sprayed 'ice blue')
- Smoke bush – *Cotinus coggygria* (Irish: tor atá faoi bhláth/tor bláthanna)
- Wild angelica – *Angelica sylvestris* (Irish: gallfheabhrán)

White, Small
- Asparagus asparagoides 'Smilax' – *Asparagus asparagoides*

White, Large
- Birch – *Betula pendula* (crainn beithe)
- Dahlia 'Café au Lait' – *Dahlia* (Irish: dáilia)
- Heleconia 'Sassy' – *Heliconia psittacorum*
- Ox-eye daisy – *Leucanthemum vulgare* (Irish: nóinín mór)

Flowers used in Link Gallery

- Allium 'Ambassador'
- Dahlia 'Café au Lait'
- Gloriosa rothschild
- Heleconia 'Sassy'
- Korean angelica
- Meadow barley – *Hordeum brachyantherum* (Irish: eorna móinéir)
- Poppy
- Wild angelica

Flowers used on stage

The flowers used here were a mix of everything we used in the Main Gallery and Link Gallery. A fitting celebration of the abundance this world has to offer.

Tawley Rock

The making of a May Day altar at Tawley Rock

Gleniff Horseshoe, County Sligo

The first time we saw Tawley Mass Rock, Co. Sligo, was when we dressed it for a wonderful wedding on a warm autumnal Friday. We had dressed the gate in orange viburnum branches, and made moss and lichen pieces to dress the altar. It was from this altar that a druid would bind the couple's hands and hearts together in matrimony.

The coming of the month of May, the shafts of speckled light amongst the bluebells swaying in a first-day-of-summer breeze, the mossed carpet marking the sacred space – it all inspired us to dress the stone tables, which stood in a row. Working under the large beech tree, the sunshine coming through was dappled by its leaves.

North-west Europe has always had a strong tradition of celebrating May Day. It was seen as a time for remembering ancient customs that, going back thousands of years, celebrated the arrival of summer whilst protecting homes against the supernatural. Wildflowers and woodland wonders, especially those in the colours of yellow and blue, are placed on altars in kitchens and churches. Be it the goddess of summer or the Virgin Mary, on that day people with evil intentions could never pass such beautiful blooms and cause harm to souls nearby.

The beech tree (*Fagus sylvatica*), or '*crann feá*' in Irish, is known as the 'Mother of the Forest', and was introduced to Ireland by the Normans. Our beech tree in this flower story has ancient, outstretched arms – a fitting inspiration for a cathedral architect – which fan out, protecting this spiritual copse of simple loveliness. The Irish god Ogma, a leading warrior of the *Tuatha Dé Danann*, and credited with the writing of the Ogham Alphabet, wrote upon beech.

Our Appassionata crew prepared the twenty-metre garland, with garland bases of green, in the studio, which was a blessing given the cold, windy weather conditions of the shoot day. Clusters of waxflower, limonium, and eucalyptus were layered as if making a large, floral rope from which to swing. Kasia and Ultan unfurled the length of flowers, attaching it to the largest branch of the beech tree. We then wove, curved, draped, and wandered the floral rope until it disappeared behind the bullaun, a stone that fills with water, as if acting as an ancient baptismal font.

We had intended to make a whole other overtly colourful piece, but the scene and the weather meant that it would be better to create a woodland sentiment. The strength of the tree's stature made us juxtapose a delicate display of seasonal flowers that fluttered in the wind before the beech – a guest at its own May Day ceremony. Yellow, fluffy mimosa, pink sweet pea, pink scabiosa (to look like our favourite sea thrift), and sky-blue larkspur were added, punctuating this garland as it meandered through a Mass Rock moment.

We saw it as an experiment in form, function and fantasy, a contemporary surrealist take on the garland dressing – as if the garland were a trick of the light that might go unnoticed when first entering this spiritual space. But if you were to draw nearer to the tree, the sacred stones, and the grouping of wild garlic and bluebells, the May Day garland would appear, a wavering spread of summer smoke. Our unorthodox floristry added a lightness of touch to this flowery necklace.

Tawley Rock

What is a Mass rock?

Mass rock sites are prolific around Ireland's countryside. They date from the era of the Penal Laws, when Catholic Mass was prohibited. This prohibition led to communities creating sacred spaces in which to celebrate Mass and other Eucharistic celebrations. Traditionally, ancient stones were taken from a church ruin and imprinted with a cross. Many of the sites were chosen because they were already considered sacred, or were nearby to a spiritual site. The majority of these Mass rocks were in fields, copses and glens; they were known to locals, and ceremony times were passed on orally so that the rituals could go on undetected. The Irish landscape became its own arena of devotion and piety during this period of persecution.

The proximity of Tawley Rock to Creevykeel (one of the largest court cairns in Ireland, and a place of governing power) within the same beech grove would suggest that the Mass rock was originally created in druidic times. The combination of the beech's spiritual symbolism and its location would lead us to believe that it was the most obvious choice for a sacred space in which to place these bullaun stones of faith.

Flowers

Flowers used in garland

- Eucalyptus – *Eucalyptus* (Irish: eoclaip)
- Larkspur – *Delphinium consolida* (Irish: deilfiniam)
- Mimosa – *Acacia dealbata* (Irish: míomós)
- Rock sea lavender – *Limonium* (Irish: lus liath aille)
- Scabiosa columbaria 'Butterfly Blue' – *Scabiosa columbaria* (Irish: cab an ghasáin)
- Sweet pea – *Lathyrus odoratus* (Irish: pis chumhra)
- Waxflower – *Chamelaucium* (Irish: bláth céarach)

Bláthanna: Irish Spaces in Flower

Altamont

A midsummer folly of roses

Tullow, County Carlow

This is a floral story about a temple of four winds, a view of three counties, a field named after sunset, a gardening heroine, and our making of a modern, midsummer herbaceous border with a twist. We wanted to create a living piece of floral art on a folly we found in a garden we fell forever in love with.

When we saw the image of a concrete, neoclassical-style folly standing at the end of steel field fences that separated two fields of cattle and ragwort, we knew that we would love to create in this space. However, as our curiosity about the location became even 'curiouser', we discovered the wonderful world of Altamont, created by an amazing Irish plantswoman and gardener, Corona North.

Altamont Gardens is outside Tullow, Co. Carlow, near the River Slaney, with majestic views of the Wicklow and Blackstairs mountains. To give you some context of where we worked, it is worth going into how the gardens of Altamont were made and why a folly was built in the eighties rather than during the post-Famine years, like most others on our island.

Corona, named after one of her father's pride hybrid rhododendrons, was a daughter of the Lecky-Watsons, who initially moved to Altamont in 1924. They had purchased this grand house and forty-acre garden from the Borror family, who had bought it from Arthur Conan Doyle's father. During the Great Famine in the mid-1800s, Dawson Borror, the son of a famous horticulturalist of the time, had one hundred men create flower beds, borders, terraces, and paths; they also built the curved staircase and made a wet meadow, which developed into a lake. This was part of a famine-relief project.

Fielding Lecky-Watson, Corona's father, was a fan of natural, wild-style planting, and also grew specimens sent down from the National Botanic Gardens, the soil of which could not support some of the planted species. However, on his passing, no one had predicted what his daughter, the plantswoman Corona North, would become, and how Altamont Gardens would evolve as one of the most diversely but passionately planted great gardens in Europe.

In an article with *The Irish Times,* Paul Cuttler, the head gardener, had the following to say of Corona and the gardens:

Mrs North loved informality and using foliage colour. She was a gatherer of plants, and spent all her time collecting and planting things she found in Irish nurseries and on her travels to England ... If she had a choice between buying a daffodil or buying a slate for the roof of the house, she would have bought a daffodil ... She had an incredible knowledge of wildlife and encouraged wildlife to stay at Altamont.

Corona married Colonel Gary North and her passion for her garden was so great that he would have to call her in for dinner with his hunting horn, stating, 'Woman's evaporated again.'

Corona passed away from illness in 1999. Her legacy includes the creation of a garden containing rare species of azaleas and camellias, space for the red squirrels and ravens in the woodland, and her harvesting of so many snowdrop varieties that there is now a wonderful annual Snowdrop Festival held every February. She also nurtured the beautiful formal gardens that are filled with midsummer bloom roses, peonies, and dahlias. What a lady to then leave this life she loved to Ireland so that we all inherited her imagination in horticulture and can enjoy the fruits of her labour in her popular Altamont Gardens.

A folly is by definition an ornamental structure – although some do have a functional purpose. They are to be viewed as part of the scenery and were usually based on the picturesque ruins of the classical world. They are often eccentric in design, and there is often an element of fantasy or make-believe in their construction. Some Irish follies were built as famine-relief projects to provide employment. Corona had her folly built in 1988 so that she could see it from her bedroom when she woke each dawn. She called it 'The Temple of Four Winds', and the counties of Carlow, Kilkenny, and Tipperary can be seen from the hill on which it sits; what's more, she named her meadow 'The Sunset Field'. Once we discovered all this, the juxtaposition and unusual scale of the folly made total sense.

As if reimagining Corona looking out her window at her folly, we thought it would be special to dress the structure with a version of her formal garden, flowering in midsummer, filled with the species she loved. She was a true fan of interplanting and mixing up species in a flower bed; she was pioneering in how she treated roses, peonies, and dahlias like shrubbery, and made them morph into bushes, thus creating more pollination. The slightly surreal setting of this neoclassical, columned temple allowed us to take classical, historical flowers such as garden and tea roses, peonies, and dahlias, and use them as accessories in a contemporary styling.

With these flowers we gathered a colour-wheel mix we loved: shades of dusty pinks, candyfloss, lavender, raspberry, magenta, crimson, and more. Exterior petals were reflexed on some flowers to add to the texture, and the fragrance of all the flower buckets meant that bees came to visit us from neighbouring fields. We positioned the colours to dissolve in gradients, from deep burgundy into dark red, tumbling into crimson and ruby and raspberry, then morphing into pinks, from bubblegum and fairy-style to whimsical and midsummer blush. The flowers grew, sprouted, tangled, but all moved along a formal structure that mirrored, in our musings, a planting idea Corona might have had. The darks and deeps seemed to add a more serious tone, but then the lightness of being in the lighter and brighter blooms made the curved roof softer in the sky.

Merging the romantic sensibility of such soft flowers in summertime with the passion of such a garden wonderland resulted in us making a strong, feminine, modern flower bed that we hoped Corona North would approve of.

Bláthanna: Irish Spaces in Flower

Flowers

Peony - *Paeonia* (Irish: piaine)

Easily the most beloved bloom we know, and
everyone's favourite flower. Its fluffy gorgeousness
starts almost in gobstopper form and then
explodes into a ball of ice-cream and joy. It takes
its name from Paeon, who studied with the god
of medicine, Asclepius. Zeus transformed Paeon
into a beautiful flower when he showed more
promise than his teacher. It means 'honour',
'wealth', and 'romance', and represents beauty
in all forms, and we love it so. It is completely
seasonal and only available from April to
July – sometimes August, if you're lucky.

Garden rose - *Rosa* x *hybrida* (Irish: rós)

Hybrid tea or garden roses are the products
of a cross between hybrid perpetual roses
and old-fashioned tea roses. They are rose
royalty, with all the loveliness you look
for in a flower: beauty and fragrance.

Hybrid teas generally produce only one
blossom at the end of each stem. The flowers on
hybrid tea roses may have over sixty petals and
can be as large as five inches across. One of their
signatures is the long, pointed buds that open by
slowly unfurling. These plants will grow anywhere
from three to six feet tall, depending on the variety
and growing conditions. Hybrid teas have been
cultivated in almost every colour except blue, with
many extraordinary bi-colours to choose from.

Flowers used in folly

Peonies used
- Peony 'Dr. Alexander Fleming'
- Peony 'Peter Brand'
- Peony 'Mothers Choice'
- Peony 'Red Charm'

Red roses used
- Rose 'Black Baccara'
- Rose 'Explorer'
- Rose 'Hearts'
- Rose 'Illusion'
- Rose 'Red Eye'
- Rose 'Red Naomi'

Pink roses used
- Rose 'Lazise'
- Rose 'Pink Avalanche'
- Rose 'Pride of Jane'
- Rose 'Secret Garden'
- Rose 'Silverstone'
- Rose 'Wild Look'

Spray roses used
- Rose spray 'Dynasty Sensation'
- Rose spray 'Mirabel'
- Rose spray 'Red Piano'
- Rose spray 'Pink Piano'

Cloghleagh Bridge

Kupala, kwiaty, wianki – a conflux of cultures, waters, and wreaths

Blessington, County Wicklow

Whether we call them *bláthanna, kwiaty,* or flowers, the joy of our working space is the opportunity it provides to learn about the cultural backgrounds of our team and, of course, our inherited flower histories. When Kasia described the Kupala Midsummer tradition from Poland, we knew that we should perform this celebration in an Irish space. Then we discovered a special spot where the Liffey and Shankill rivers meet under the Cloghleagh Bridge – a confluence of Dublin and Wicklow – before moving towards the Poulaphouca Reservoir. What followed was a flower love story during summer solstice.

First, a few words on the Slavic tradition of Kupala. On the shortest night of the year – the turn of 23–24 June, or St John's Eve – pagan people would celebrate the solstice by delighting in fire, water, fertility, and joy. *Wianki,* or wreaths, were wound with wildflowers of the midsummer season, and girls would float them in a river, trying to read the fortune of future relationships in their flowing pattern. That is, if they didn't sink.

Sometimes men would try and capture a maiden's wreath as a way of capturing their heart. What is even more special about the tradition is that the eve of Ivan Kupala was believed to be the only time of year that a mystical fern would bloom. If found by a lucky fern-seeker, prosperity, luck, discernment, and power would befall them. By complete coincidence, there is an ancient Irish belief that the finder of a special fern seed would be granted the gift of being good at cards and also rendered invisible.

The next part of the Kupala custom is our favourite. Traditionally, the village virgins or unmarried women, their status signified by the wearing of hair garlands, would enter the forest in search of the aforementioned fern flower. The village men – their suitors – would follow. The unfurling of this fern flower symbolised the blossoming of love amidst the magical depths of the forest. The rest is left to the imagination.

Midsummer making

Midsummer is always a time of ripened, voluptuous flowers. It is the season when we see buckets of colour, from the dustiest hues of blue and pink to bright greens, adding liveliness, and the punkiness of corals and fuschias punching through; carpets of peonies in all their ice-cream forms, sweet peas reaching their full glory, garden roses spoiling us with their unfurlings each day. The best thing is that the fragrances are so full at this time of year. There was a magical, unbridled joy amongst our team when asked to make their favourite summer flower crowns. Every one of our floristas came up with something different, reflecting their own styles and taste, basing their ideas on the flowers' meanings, histories and emotions.

Letting the crowns go

To stand on the mossy, lichened banks of the River Liffey as it pools and swirls beneath emerald-green oaks and moss peat is a meditative experience. We carefully climbed down below the bridge, trying to find the spot where the wreaths should first be thrown. Wellies and wetsuits were worn, which didn't do much to evoke the maidens throwing their love *wianki* to the river passage. Midges were burning our scalps, but the setting worked. Sunlight streamed in pockets through the whispering green canopy of oak and beech; moss carpets stretched down to the water; the river was so clear that we could see every pebble waiting to be picked up for skimming.

    We stood at the base of the bridge, balancing on the slippy, emerald-sheened rocks, holding poles. Ultan placed each wreath just beyond the fall of a delicate waterfall, which sent each headband swirling around and around. Kupala is all about the journey of the floral wreath; we watched as they whirled, dipped, drowned, and wobbled until they reached downstream, where the water current accelerated in speed. After the wreaths' journey under the bridge, they arrived in velvet-sheened river water and a wooded wonderland with gnarled ancient oak trees full of midsummer greens, their roots spreading like tendrils you had to avoid tripping over. Here, the river opened up into multiple streams, all moving fast until they reached large groupings of rocks that interrupted the river's flow and created rockpools. This waylaid some wreaths, which wound around and around in the whirl. Others pushed on with the current, on through the sunlight to new waterways ahead.

    This floral story allowed us to untether our imagination and create a setting for love to be found. We might not have found any flowering magical ferns that day, but the stillness of staying in the surrounds of water, woods, and birdsong allowed us all to bask in a new adventure.

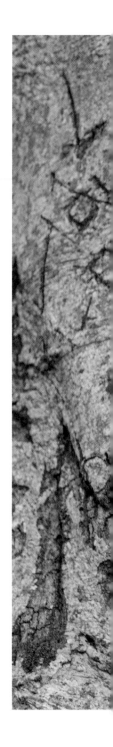

Cloghleagh Bridge

Flowers

**Royal fern – *Osmunda regalis*
(Irish: raithneach ríúil)**

The fern is a fairy plant here in Ireland due to its reputation in Irish folklore. We found out that a fairy changeling would turn into a clump of fern when banished. Another magical quality of the plant in Irish myth has to do with the fact that it bears neither flowers nor fruit, but produces mysterious seeds called spores. In the tale *Táin Bó Cúailnge,* 'The Cattle Raid of Cooley', the warrior Nera enters a fairy mound on Samhain; because it's summer in fairyland, he returns from the mound with armfuls of wild fern, garlic, and primrose. Excavations of Viking Dublin also show that ferns were used for bedding and thatching. However, it was not used in folk medicine, as it is poisonous when brewed!

Flowers used in *wianki*

- Blue star milkweed – *Oxypetalum coeruleum* (Irish: dúlamán réalta gorm)
- Bluebell – *Hyacinthoides non-scripta* (Irish: coinnle corra)
- Dog-rose – *Rosa canina* (Irish: feirdhris)
- Forget-me-not – *Myosotis* (Irish: lusán na néan)
- Garden Cosmos – *Cosmos bipinnatus*
- Gentiana – *Gentiana verna* (Irish: ceadharlach bealtaine)
- Larkspur – *Delphinium consolida* (Irish: sála fuiseoige)
- Lisianthus 'Alissa Pink' – *Eustoma grandiflorum* (Irish: coinnle corra)
- Ox-eye daisy – *Leucanthemum vulgare* (Irish: nóinín mór)
- Peony 'Coral Sunset' – *Paeonia* (Irish: piaine)
- Pistachia – *Pistacia lentiscus* (Irish: crann piostáisí)
- Ranunculus 'Cloni Folkers'
- Ranunculus 'Cloni Mandarino'
- Ranunculus 'Cloni Venere'
- Ranunculus 'Super Alaska'
- Rosehip 'Corallo' (Irish: mogóir róis)
- Rose spray 'Miss Bombastic' (Irish: rós)
- Royal fern – *Osmunda regalis* (Irish: raithneach ríúil)
- Viburnum opulus 'Compactum' – *Viburnum opulus* (Irish: caor chon)
- Waxflower – *Chamelaucium* (Irish: bláth céarach)
- White delphinium 'El Dewi Siberia' – *Delphinium grandiflorum* (Irish: deilfiniam)
- White delphinium 'Volkerfried'
- White Lilac – *Syringa vulgaris* (Irish: líológ)
- White peony 'Duchesse de Nemour' – *Paeonia* (Irish: piaine)

The Museum Building, Trinity College

An unexpected vision of symmetry

College Green, Dublin 2

'There's no symmetry in nature. One eye is never exactly the same as the other. There's always a difference. We all have a more or less crooked nose and an irregular mouth.'

Édouard Manet

Our studio is ten minutes away from our city centre flower shop when walking at a pace. We go back and forth between these locations on most days, and a pleasurable way to spend this time is to walk through the grounds of Trinity College. And as we walk past the playing fields and turn right beside the rose garden, where the bountiful blossom tree sits, we always marvel at the symmetrical building beside it. This is the Museum Building, and it has housed the departments of geology, geography, and engineering for one hundred and fifty years. However, unless you studied at Trinity or visited as a tourist, you might never have realised that it's there, and quite how special it is.

This landmark Victorian building was the first place we thought of when the concept of a book about flowers in Irish spaces came into focus. Its creation in the 1850s marked the first time that geology and architecture came together; the materials used represent an Irish geological lesson in themselves. The first time we went to an event here, it was sheer reverence that we felt for this almost sacramental space – and then there was the wonderment when we entered the arched, wooden doorway and met the frame of an ancient Irish elk. We felt blessed to be allowed to look around this space amidst the many students for whom the Museum Building is simply an everyday college faculty building.

The Museum Building, Trinity College

2nd Lieut. David Ryle, R.E. killed
in action, France, May 19th 1915.

The purpose of the Museum Building was three-fold. First, it was to provide the staff with offices and teaching spaces, and include the engineering and geological museum galleries. Second, the building, through the efforts of the architects and the college board, was to promote indigenous Irish decorative stone and carving craftsmanship at a time that saw an increased awareness of Ireland's natural resources. Third, through the placement of decorative stone columns and naturalistic carvings, it was to serve as a permanent repository and source of information on the geology, flora, and fauna of Ireland – as such, it functioned as an oversized museum display.

While the richly coloured marbles and intricately carved capitals on the top of the columns of the Museum Building instil a sense of wonderment in visitors, they also shout out for a recognition and appreciation of Ireland's native talent and natural resources. These carvings, both inside and outside the building, remain the most significant legacy of what is likely the most talented team of stone-carvers that Ireland has ever produced. This pioneering and experimental building was the result of a uniquely forward-thinking partnership between the Deane & Woodward architectural practice, the O'Sheas, renowned for their talent as mason sculptors, and a supportive, risk-taking university board. Conceived at a time of increased nationalistic pride, it coincided with the development of technologies necessary for the fabrication of decorative stone columns, and, most importantly, the revival of artisan craftsmanship.

It is unusual that so much was put into the design, but these were the unique circumstances that enabled it – and this is why we wanted to shoot here. This floral story is all about our attempt to create symmetry: a rhythmic repetition of flower pieces, all carrying a likeness in shape and nature, to fill the imperial staircase with the ceremony it deserves.

In the front hall we delicately balanced lupins, foxgloves, eremurus, mona lavender, and moss on each of the steps to make a voluptuous, natural frame that continued up the staircase. We created each flowering section in a stylised, symmetrical way to integrate simply with the earthy Connemara marble tones, the fossil-full Kilkenny limestone, and the still-life-carved animations of Irish garden and wildflower elements on each of the fifteen pillared columns. The drama of the curved wall detail, the double-domed, Byzantine-style roof of coloured brick in Mediterranean palettes of red, yellow and blue, the large pendulum-swinging clock – it all allowed the building to become the perfect stage for our staircase series. The two fanned sets of arches above the right side of the staircase had tall, floral displays placed amongst them, as if acting as trumpets heralding a new royal arrival. Working here, we were able to create in a building that is devoted to knowing everything about the stone and soil our native flora grow in – a community for the expert geologists, botanists, and geographers who work to discover how our own island is faring in terms of its roots, earth, and self.

This unique, unusual, but astounding space is home to a cultural community, be they department heads, lecturers, painters, minders, librarians, technicians, or any number of other occupations. We think we met just about everyone that day, each person with their own story about what this building meant to them. Perhaps it was the first time that we realised how our work was a kind of visual poetry for everyone who crossed our path; that our craft was simply another way of making this botanical conservatory more beautiful on a Friday in June.

Bláthanna: Irish Spaces in Flower

Flowers

Flowers used in Museum Building

- Foxtail lily – *Eremurus cleopatra*
  (Irish: lile sionnach)
- Lupins – *Lupinus* (Irish: lúipín crua)
- Foxglove – *Digitalis purpurea*
  (Irish: lus mór)
- Plectranthus 'Mona Lavender'
  – *Plectranthus*

Bláthanna: Irish Spaces in Flower

Hunting Brook

Ombré dining in a forest glen

Blessington, County Wicklow

'The beauty of a cloud or a flower lies
in its unconscious unfolding of itself.'

Kakuzo Okakura

Extract from *Ideals of the East*

'Everything you do in making a garden should be a containment of the heart.'

The Venerable Myoko-ni

Extract from *The Japanese Garden*

We borrowed a wonderful forest glen from Jimi Blake, whose home, Hunting Brook Gardens, hosts one of the best private plant collections in Ireland. We wanted to make a single-flower table centrepiece in order to experiment with an ombré of colours and tones, all using hydrangea. The gardens, located in Blessington, Co. Wicklow, were a perfect opportunity. Although we daily tell our lovely brides and clients that flowers do not come in definitive pantone colours, we picked each colour by sight on a live-time flower market auction to see if we could make the tones fade up and down according to our liking.

We walked through an amphitheatre of colourful planted combinations in the beds around Jimi's timber house, situated in his voluminous garden. Jimi has a wonderful eye; his choice of plants paints a picture in his garden. They are characters to him, and it is his perception of how they relate to each other, depend on each other, and grow that makes this curated botanical playground a creative, successful ecosystem.

The vocabulary of rooms is frequently applied to gardens and it is true that they share many attributes. At the same time, the elemental nature of a garden is its essence. However small and inwardly focused a green space may be, we do not want to forget that we are outdoors, subject to the vicissitudes of the weather, the changing seasons and the quality of the light, where the relationship between things is constantly being redrawn by the cycles of growth and decay.

John Pawson

Extract from *The Japanese Garden*

A wonderful meal at a large outdoors table is always the summer goal. Table centrepieces are made to fill a space along the centre and brighten a guest's eye. We decided to let this dining space evolve with our meandering ombré hydrangea. A giant fluffy cloud of chicken wire was moulded and meticulously fashioned to softly resemble a childlike, large cumulus shape. We laid out the hydrangea stems, working out a system so that blues, pinks, purples, reds, and burgundies travelled in tone, hue, and texture. Then it was a matter of making each colour section sing, manoeuvring each single stem to suit the wavering of the wire base. Hydrangea is not usually used alone in a garland-style table dressing, but we felt that the cloud-shaped heads would add a sculptural definition and fitting contrast to the elemental setting.

The hydrangea colours punctuated the space of this forest glen garden. Bands of sunlight dappled the darks and lights so that every shade popped in a Sirkian technicolour, a beautiful variation to the deep, dense greens. It seemed a shame that it was only to be the once that we sat and ate lunch at our new favourite ombré-styled table setting amongst the summer glades.

Bláthanna: Irish Spaces in Flower

Flowers

Hydrangea – *Hydrangea macrophylla*
(**Irish: hiodrainsia**)

First introduced to Europe, in the 1800s, from Japan, these very thirsty pompom-shaped flowers are named after water barrels – the Greek *hydor* meaning 'water', and *angos* meaning 'jar' or 'vessel'. Treasured for their boldness and delicacy, they symbolise heartfelt emotions both good and bad. The flower head's colour ranges from the whitest of white, to pink, to blue, to green, to purple, to burgundy – all in shades of dusty to punky, the shade completely depending on the acidity level of the soil that the hydrangea grows in.

It is such a useful, effective flower for any florist to use in their work, and we love the fact that by drying them upside down in hydrangea headstands we get to keep looking at them all year round.

Flowers used in table centrepiece

- Hydrangea 'Elbtal Classic' – *Hydrangea* (Irish: hiodrainsia)
- Hydrangea 'Magical Coral'
- Hydrangea 'Magical Emerald Classic'
- Hydrangea 'Magical Greenfire'
- Hydrangea 'Magical Ruby Aubergine'
- Hydrangea 'Magical Ruby Red'
- Hydrangea 'Marspein Blue'
- Hydrangea 'Pimpernel Blue'
- Hydrangea 'Rodeo Purple'
- Hydrangea 'Rodeo Purple Classic'
- Hydrangea 'Rodeo Red'
- Hydrangea 'Smiley Blue'
- Hydrangea 'Verena Blue'
- Hydrangea 'Verena Roze Groot'

Corke Lodge

An inside-out garden

Woodbrook, County Wicklow

'One arranges flowers as the spirit moved you; to obey some inner prompting to put this colour with that, to have brilliance here, line there, a sense of opulence in this place or sparseness in that; to suit your surroundings, your mood, the weather, the occasion. In a word, to do as you please, just as, if you could, paint a picture.'

Constance Spry

One of the great privileges in our flower world is that we get to dress houses and homes, all filled and coloured in different ways to suit the people that live in them. Suddenly, a stage is set for flowers to simply accessorise and add abundance so that a hall feels more welcoming, a table divinely decorated; the scent of even a basic flower arrangement is enough to fill a home with joy.

We discovered Corke Lodge – in the words of Jane Power, a 'dreamlike place minutes from modernity' – by way of the garden it sits in, designed and minded by Alfred Cochrane, hidden away between Shankill and Bray in Dublin. Alfred is firstly an architect; he designs gardens from a visual point of view so that everything looks fabulous from the first day of planting. Stone follies sit along clipped boxwood and ferns; it is an aisle of green that meets with a neatly situated bench, perfectly placed for a morning coffee accompanied by the neighbour's white cat.

I got interested in the garden, not particularly liking flowers. I do like them but am not an expert on growing them; my gardens are architectural pieces, they are shapes, they are greens, so my garden is where I experiment on and most of my gardens are the same: clipped cypress trees, palm trees and more.

Alfred Cochrane

The star of the garden is the cork oak tree (*Quercus suber*), the largest in Ireland – Alfred believes that it was planted by the original owners, the Magan family, as a joke. The estate was originally called Corke Lodge because it was built upon a marsh, which is '*corcorach*' in Irish, and perhaps Lord Magan and his architect William Farrell thought it ironic to plant such a Mediterranean specimen in the boggy ground; they had wanted to make an olive grove but could only find the cork tree. Three centuries of land drainage have dried the soil adequately to allow for this giant of a tree to star in its own show; sitting amidst a wealthy lush of green, it is the centrepiece of the garden's design.

But then we entered Alfred's house and instantly knew that, as Constance once declared, we had to 'obey some inner prompting' and create within a space of such personality. First of all, the house was designed for entertaining. Whether it is the fact that Charles Dickens got the inspiration for *Great Expectations'* Miss Havisham from Augusta Magan – a previous resident who was jilted the night before her wedding day and sat in her wedding dress in front of her wedding breakfast for forty years – or that Katharine Hepburn and Geraldine Fitzgerald both resided here at different times, this home holds histories that fascinated us from before our arrival. Alfred, who has a Lebanese and Irish background, inherited the house in the eighties and decided to present his home as a restoration showcase.

Here are the roses
That know all about people,
And yet are still filled with love.
True, they have thorns that tear.
But we forgive them
for their lovely humanity.
They suit us:
They have lived with us so long.
When the others have gone
they will still be here,
sending up strong sustaining branches
through the thicket of our lives.
They are familiar faces:
They give us a sense of security.

David Austin
'Roses'

The function of a dining room is likely to be a thing of the past before long, but Corke Lodge's beautifully decadent dining room is filled with a lifetime's worth of collected objects and antiques that serve to make it whole. Purchased bit by bit from Paul Cooke's antique shop on Francis Street, the room is furnished with Roman architectural illustrations and paintings, antique consoles and sideboards, a Turkish rug, and a wonderful glass and iron table surrounded by sixteen dining chairs; a second door balances out the room, as per Alfred's symmetrical focus.

This dining room, by order of its own divination, allowed us to dress it with spring flowers, which acted as a chorus in our swansong to David Austin, the famed rose breeder, who passed away in December 2018.

Austin created more than two hundred and forty types of new roses, and over twenty-four years he won many gold medals at the Chelsea Flower Show. His scented hybrid tea roses give us so much joy when they arrive, individually packaged so that every petal is preserved to perfection. His legacy lies not only in the varieties that he originated, created through amazing perseverance and belief in his breeding capabilities, but also in the happiness his flowers bring to so many occasions in the circle of life, from births to marriages – celebrations of all there is to celebrate. It is always a privilege to work with such beautiful flowers, especially given today's penchant for hothouse-bred flowers, which lose their scent along their journey.

We worked in a rhythm together, bumping colours of pink, raspberry, ruby, and red the day before the photo shoot. As if instructed, the roses all opened their hearts and burst out the beauty bred by David Austin, creating an uneven but measured display along each side of the long table. We playfully sprinkled 'Yves Piaget' roses, myosotis and ranunculus amongst the rosy mix to add further richness to this space. Guests at this dinner party included the identical golden roosters sat at either side of the mantlepiece, and an array of hellebores and pretty fritillaria, onlookers to the rose dinner party at the dining table.

We adorned the glass table with a meandering candle holder, its colour emulating the gilded roosters, its shape a trope of Austin's: a meandering river as the embodiment of nature's beauty. As Gearoid Muldowney of Superfolk so fittingly put it, 'The meandering river is the embodiment of all that is simple and beautiful in nature. The river gently navigates the landscape. Its path is constantly improving and evolving. It is calm and restless at same time.' Through these meanderings and rich blossoms, our flower structures brought the beauty of nature into Alfred Cochrane's symmetrically driven home.

'Do whatever you please, follow your own star; be original if you want to be and don't if you don't want to be. Just be natural and gay and light hearted and pretty and simple and overflowing and general and baroque and bare and austere and stylised and wild and daring and conservative, and learn and learn and learn. Open your mind to every form of beauty.'

Constance Spry

The drawing room is Alfred's favourite; every element of its decoration is a semblance of his work. Frescoes painted on the wall are inspired by the garden's 'Irish exotica', the palms and lush green visible through the windows. The space is occupied by a mix of antique and Cochrane-designed furniture, their American, striped fabric of a quality that it has held its vibrancy in colour and tone in face of the sunlight.

We mixed in spring beech, hornbeam, larch and ivy with jungle-style palms and rose vines. Then we placed orange fritillaria to stand amidst the Irish Mediterranean gardenscape, as if disco-dancing in the room. Pops of sunshine-orange mirrored the meticulously painted frescoes on the wall.

The balanced, symmetrical, tall glass windows set the stage on either side of the majestic mantelpiece. The reception room was filled with an exotic garden elegance, as if ready for the best pre-dinner cocktails in town. For us, this was a way to combine Alfred's visions of gardener, architect, and designer into one.

The secondary reception room looks out on the grandeur of the centre-stage cork oak. Low seat windows frame the room on either side of a Victorian mantelpiece. Usually we have to dress these spaces with vases, candles or garlands of bloom and foliage. This time, inspired by Alfred's love of lush green, an explosion of green amaranth burst from the mantelpiece over the fireplace, complemented by hellebores still hanging around after the long winter season. Amaranthus has a way of adding a raw elegance as it sits, spiralised, as if it had gone through a pasta maker. And as though guests were following a theme for a dinner party, the painting above the mantelpiece is an artist's impression of the drawing room next door.

We filled the windowsills with black fritillaria; they curved, waved, and swayed amidst their moss beds, with a green background from the fern plants just outside. The famous cork oak, huge in the near-distance, almost looked like it wanted to join all the flower fun inside. A first edition chair, designed by Alfred for a New York art gallery, sits nonchalantly amidst the flora drama, not looking in the least out of place.

Flowers

Magnolia leaves – *Magnolia*
(Irish: magnóilia)

The heralding of spring arrives with magnolia flowers blooming in gardens all over Dublin; they also mark the month before we might start to see fluffy cherry blossoms. Named after the French botanist Pierre Magnol, these flowers are pollinated by beetles. We used their leaves in the front drawing room for their presence: their elegant, almond-shaped leaves add such texture. We sometimes make door wreaths with the copper-shade underside in autumn. Then, when the flowers and leaves disappear for winter, we love to use their furry-bud twiggery to create drama in tall displays.

Ivy – *Hedera*
(Irish: eidhneán)

As florists, if we see a wall covered in long lengths of glossy ivy, our hearts beat that bit faster. Yes, we use it to dress our wreaths, fill our bouquets, and green up our garlands, but it's the texture, especially of its berries, that adds a luxurious feel to anything we make in winter; it is traditionally used for decoration around Christmas in Ireland. In Irish folk culture, it was used as a cure for corns, coughs, and colds, but it is also a symbol of life and enduring fertility due to its clinging nature, making a home of whichever surface will allow.

Forget-me-not – *Myosotis*
(Irish: lus míonla goirt)

This flower is a symbol of love, faithfulness and friendship. It derives from the borage family and we love using it so.

Flowers used in drawing room

- Alocasia – *Alocasia sanderiana* (Irish: alocasia)
- Areca palm – *Dypsis lutescens* (Irish: crann airice)
- Eucalyptus – *Eucalyptus cinerea* (Irish: eoclaip)
- Imperial fritillary – *Fritillaria imperialis* (Irish: fritileán)
- Ivy
- Magnolia leaves – *magnolia* (Irish: magnóilia)
- Willow peppermint – *Eucalyptus nicholii*

Flowers used in dining room

- Forget-me-not – *Myosotis* (Irish: lus míonla goirt)
- Fritillaria monantha – *Fritillaria monantha*
- Guinea flower – *Fritillaria meleagris*
- Hellebore 'Penny's Pink' (Irish: ealabairín)
- Hellebore 'Magnificent Bells'
- Persian buttercups – *Ranunculus asiaticus* (Irish: ranúncalas)
- Ranunculus 'Rose Venere'
- Ranunculus 'Azur Black'
- Rose 'Bridesmaid' – Rosa (Irish: rós)

- Rose 'Bubblegum'
- Rose 'Candy Avalanche'
- Rose 'David Austin Edith'
- Rose 'David Austin Keira'
- Rose 'David Austin Miranda'
- Rose 'David Austin Purity'
- Rose 'Glorious'
- Rose 'Lullaby'
- Rose 'Memory Lane'
- Rose 'Mirabel'
- Rose 'Mother of Pearl'
- Rose 'Odilia'
- Rose 'Patchouli'
- Rose 'Pearl Avalanche'
- Rose 'Pink Avalanche'
- Rose 'Red Elegance'
- Rose 'Red Naomi'
- Rose 'Secret Garden'
- Rose 'Yves Piaget'
- Rose 'Espana'
- Rose 'Ladykiller'
- Rose 'Smeralda Show'

Flowers used in secondary reception

- Green amaranth – *Amaranthus hybridus* (Irish: amarantus)
- Fritillaria persica – *Fritillaria persica*

Bibliography & Acknowledgements

Can we say a million thanks to all of you for all of the Appassionata Flowers love over the last fifteen years. Without your flower following, we would not be here, and we appreciate you all, our lovely customers, so much.

A book is created by a community. Without Stephanie Boner, Maeve Convery and Ronan Colgan, this book would not have been born or published. Thank you for everything and for making our dream come true.

To David Wall, Kayleigh McCarthy, and the magical team in WorkGroup, you brought it all together in such a beautiful way – you are just brilliant.

Myles McCionnaith – After seeing our words transformed by your detailed magic, we can't thank you enough for all the hard work you did.

A big thank you, from Ruth especially, to John Redmond, Rosie McMeel and Louise Stokes for being such amazing sounding boards and supportive friends.

To Iseult, Yvette and Sean's gorgeous daughter and our niece, thank you for all your fairy flower help in Sligo.

Aisling Farinella, thank you for making us look ourselves in a glamorous way. Your eye is fantastic. We loved how you brought out our personalities through your design and styling genius.

Jennifer Quinn, a million thanks for looking after us in hair, faces and fun on our shoot day.

We also so appreciated the luxury of being lent such beautiful clothing from Havana, Costume, Indigo & Cloth and Brown Thomas. Such a pleasure to wear Simone Rocha, Cecilie Bahnsen, Dries Van Noten, Celine, Alexander McQueen, Finery, Paul Smith, and more. We felt fabulous that shoot day.

To all of our parents – we promise to visit you so much more from now on and thank you for all your love and support.

Thank you to all of our families and friends for bearing with us while we dived down deep into our flower world; we promise you that we will see you all again from now on.

Altamont: A midsummer folly of roses

Kleiner, Fred S., *Gardner's Art through the Ages: The Western Perspective, Volume II* (Boston, 2016).

'Tullow's glory is garden paradise gifted to nation', *Irish Times*, https://www.irishtimes.com/life-and-style/homes-and-property/tullow-s-glory-is-garden-paradise-gifted-to-nation-1.264772 [accessed 10 September 2019].

Acknowledgements

A big thanks to Pauline Dowling and Liam Ó Culbáird from the wonderful OPW team in Altamont, and Robin Harvey.

Carrowmore: A flower gate of folklore where the land meets the sky

Bulfin, William, *Rambles in Eirinn* (Dublin, 1908).

Mac Coitir, Niall, *Irish Wild Plants: Myths, Legends & Folklore* (Cork, 2008).

Yeats, William Butler, *The Collected Works of W. B. Yeats: Volume I: The Poems* (2nd edn, New York, 2010).

Acknowledgements

The OPW

Corke Lodge: An inside-out garden

Austin, David, *The Breathing Earth* (London, 2014).

Mac Coitir, Niall, *Irish Wild Plants: Myths, Legends & Folklore* (Cork, 2008).

Powers, Jane, and Jonathan Hession, *The Irish Garden* (London, 2015).

Spry, Constance, *Constance Spry's Garden Notebook* (New York, 1940).

Spry, Constance, *Flower Decoration* (Chicago, 1993).

Acknowledgements

Alfred Cochrane – we are so grateful to you for letting us cover your home in flowers and foliage for two days. You are such a gentleman, and we just adored being in your home and garden. It has been so wonderful to get to know you. Thank you so much.

Brian – thank you for all of your help in helping us find this treasure of a home.

Glendalough: A currach botanica

Yeats, William Butler, *Essays and Introductions* (London, 1961).

Acknowledgements

Thank you, Ann Fitzpatrick (Conservation Ranger, Wicklow Mountains National Park), for trusting us with the key to the park and for all the help in organising the shoot.

A big thanks to Ross of Boyne Boats for being such a legend that day. It was amazing to have you there with us, along with the beautiful boat you made.

Hunting Brook: Ombré dining in a forest glen

Blake, Jimi, and Noel Kingsbury, *A Beautiful Obsession: Jimi Blake's World of Plants at Hunting Brook Gardens* (2019).

Okakura, Kakuzo, *Ideals of the East: The Spirit of Japanese Art* (Mineola, 2012).

Walker, Sophie, *The Japanese Garden* (London, 2017).

Acknowledgements

Jimi Blake — for having the most wonderful gardens for us to play in and an enthusiasm for our book.

Huntington: A daydream swing

Bunbury, Turtle, 'Huntington Castle: Ghostly Tales & Worthy Fellowships', http://www.turtlebunbury.com/history/history_houses/hist_hse_huntington.html [accessed 10 September 2019].

Carroll, Lewis, *The Complete Illustrated Works of Lewis Carroll* (1996).

Mac Coitir, Niall, *Irish Trees: Myths, Legends and Folklore* (Cork, 2015).

Acknowledgements

A million thanks to Alexander Durdin Robertson for a fabulous lunch and for hosting us that day.

Earlsfort Place: Weekly working flowers making a workplace sing

Crawford, Ilse, *A Frame for Life* (New York, 2014).

De Vries, James, 'Life's Work : An Interview with Marc Newson', *Harvard Business Review*, https://hbr.org/2015/01/lifes-work-marc-newson [accessed 10 September 2019].

Acknowledgements

A special thank you to Niall Gaffney and Anita O'Rourke for organising and permitting access to shoot in IPUT's building on Earlsfort Terrace.

King's Inns: A stairwell of smoke bush

Acknowledgements

We are indebted to Claire Hanley and all at King's Inns for allowing us to take over their stairway on such a hot, sunny day. And Edmundo, how brilliant you were that day.

Mullaghmore: A Mullaghmore light melody

Barry, Kevin, *Beatlebone* (London, 2015).

Acknowledgements

Thank you to my parents, Eileen and Ray Monahan, for allowing us take over their special space in Mullaghmore for a day.

Restaurant Patrick Guilbaud: An experiential orchestra we love

Ryan, Susan, and Barry McCall, *Restaurant Patrick Guilbaud: The First Thirty Years* (Dublin, 2011).

Acknowledgements

Thank you Stéphane, Patrick, and Guillaume for always supporting us and for allowing us to photograph in your beautiful restaurant on such a busy day.

Streedagh Strand: A faerie land gate on a gusty day

Kiberd, Declan, and P.J. Mathews, *Handbook of the Irish Revival: An Anthology of Irish Cultural and Political Writings 1891–1922* (Notre Dame, 2016).

The Front Room: An indoor meadow reflects in resin

Jarrett, Keith, *The Köln Concert* (ECM 1064/65 ST, 1975) [incl. sleeve notes].

The Fumbally: Happenings in green

Campbell, Joseph, *The Power of Myth* (New York, 1988).

Mac Coitir, Niall, *Irish Wild Plants: Myths, Legends & Folklore* (Cork, 2008).

Acknowledgements

Thank you to Luca and Aisling for giving over your precious spaces.

The RHA: A Tetris time moment

Brown, Box, *Tetris: The Games People Play* (London, 2016).

Acknowledgements

A million thanks to Patrick T. Murphy and Vanessa Moss, who gave us free rein and true artistic licence.

Cloghleagh Bridge: *Kupala, kwiaty, wianki* — a conflux of cultures, waters, and wreaths

Acknowledgements

To Shadow, Yvette and Sean's dog, who jumped around playfully as the midges burned our scalps.

The Westbury Hotel: Studies in seasons

Acknowledgements

A million thanks to Bernie Gallagher, Pat King, Vincent O'Gorman, and all of the fantastic team in the Westbury, who allowed us to play flowers whenever we needed to.

The Museum Building, Trinity College: An unexpected vision of symmetry

Casey, Christine, and Patrick Wyse Jackson, eds, *The Museum Building of Trinity College Dublin: A Model of Victorian Craftsmanship* (Dublin, 2019).

Acknowledgements

Thank you to the Trinity Estates and Facilities Office for allowing us to take over your building for a day. Thanks also to Mary Foody, and to all of the academic team we met that day, who were all so interesting to speak with. And a massive thank you to Patrick N. Wyse Jackson, who gave us so much information on the Museum Building.

VISUAL Carlow: Let the gardens grow

Acknowledgments

We couldn't have created here without the wonderful input from Emma Lucy O'Brien, Director of VISUAL, and her friendly and supportive team. What a wonderful place to spend a day, in amongst such inspirational design and exhibitions. Thank you also to Daphne Wright for allowing us have your amazing art piece in our book.

Bláthanna, the Irish for 'flowers', is such a simple word. This book, however, is a testament to the magic that can be conveyed when artistic vision meets a deep knowledge of flora, and an inherent understanding of space. *Bláthanna* is a stunning curation of floral short stories in exceptional spaces, the length and breadth of Ireland. Drawing from Irish countryside textures and seasonal blooms, elegant rooms and magnificent exteriors, this anthology shows how creativity with flowers can be inspired and reimagined.

This work reveals the essence of floral traditions, legends, and histories to showcase the beauty that can be created all around us. The team behind renowned Dublin florists Appassionata Flowers have gifted us with a floral lens through which to view this amazing landscape we call home. A combination of wonderful and consistently surprising artistry, breath-taking photography, and poetic, thoughtful writing makes *Bláthanna* a joyous celebration of floristry, and of Ireland itself.